Donald R. McQueen

CANADIAN NATIONAL STEAM!

Volume 2: Road Numbers

1 to 50	— various	— Class X
100 to 172	— 4-4-0	— Class A
212 to 399	— 4-4-0	— Class B
Newfoundland Railway		

For Dianne (1942-2008)

Railfare DC Books

ABOUT THE AUTHOR

Don McQueen
[ROBERT RIEHL PHOTOGRAPHY]

Don McQueen, born in Toronto in 1938, was raised in Brockville, Ontario and received an Honour Arts degree in History from Queen's University in 1963. Moving to London, Ontario later that same year, he began a secondary school teaching career which spanned 33 years in six of the city's schools. Initially a school librarian, teaching Canadian history and geography, Don also taught and developed school curricula in the humanities, world civilizations, law, sociology, world issues, and photography.

His interest in Canadian railway history developed at an early age, although not as early as his fascination with all forms of transportation, especially trains. Brockville, both a St. Lawrence River town and a terminal for two Canadian transcontinental railways, provided a lure which was impossible to resist. His articles, background research or contributions have appeared in a number of Canadian books and publications, including *Branchline*, *CN Lines* (Canadian National Railways Historical Association), *Canadian Rail*, *Extra 2200 South*, *Kingston Rail*, *Locomotive Notes II*, Ontario Northland Railway Historical & Technical Society's *The Northlander*, and Upper Canada Railway Society's *Newsletter / Rail & Transit*. In other railway related themes, he has written illustrated articles in the *Toy Train Operating Society Bulletin* (Marx tinplate toy trains) and in *Freight Cars Journal* (a White Pass & Yukon rolling stock roster).

Constructed in Kingston is Don's premier Canadian railway history reference to date, co-authored with Bill Thomson. That volume chronicled the history, in text and image, of the Canadian Locomotive Companies of Kingston from 1854 to 1968. Now out of print, that book remains a standard source in Canadian locomotive railway history.

Living in London, another railway city, resulted in a keen interest in locomotive production at General Motors' Canadian locomotive manufacturing facility. After becoming one of the charter members in the creation of the Forest City Railway Society in 1968, he continued his commitment as one of the editors of the organization's monthly publication, *Tempo Jr.*, and created a daily electronic digest, *Froth*.

When time permitted during his career, as well as in retirement, he paced his research with another of his passions – photography. In addition to his images appearing in the above periodicals, others have been published in several books such as *Signatures in Steel*, the reissued *Narrow Gauge Railways of Canada*, *Self-Propelled Cars of the CNR* and several Morning Sun publications including *Chesapeake & Ohio in Color* and various rolling stock volumes.

In retirement, Don keeps busier than ever with all of the above pursuits, including his iris garden in London, Ontario and with his family, Heather, "Socs", Christopher and Danielle.

Book designed and typeset in Adobe Garamond Pro, ITC Garamond, and Myriad MM.
Overall book design by Ian Cranstone, Osgoode, Ontario.
Graphic grid designed by Primeau & Barey, Montreal, Quebec.
Printed and bound in Canada.

Legal Deposit, *Bibliothèque et Archives nationales du Québec* and the National Library of Canada, 3rd Trimester, 2013.

Library and Archives Canada Cataloguing in Publication

McQueen, Donald R., 1938-
Canadian National Steam! / Donald R. McQueen.

Includes bibliographical references and indexes.
ISBN 978-1-927599-00-6 (Premiere vol. : pbk.).—ISBN 978-1-927599-01-3 Premiere vol. : bound).—ISBN 978-1-927599-02-0 (v. 2).—
ISBN 978-1-927599-03-7 (v. 3).—ISBN 978-1-927599-04-4 (v. 4).—
ISBN 978-1-927599-05-1 (v. 5).—ISBN 978-1-927599-06-8 (v. 6).—
ISBN 978-1-927599-07-5 (v. 7).—ISBN 978-1-927599-08-2 (v. 8).—
ISBN 978-1-927599-09-9 (set)

1. Steam Locomotives—Canada—History. 2. Canadian National Railways—History. I. Title.

TJ603.4.C32C34 2013 625.26'10971 C2013-900857-8

We acknowledge the financial support of the Government of Canada through the Book Publishing Industry Development Program (BPIDP) for our publishing activities.

For our publishing activities, **Railfare DC Books** gratefully acknowledges the financial support of The Canada Council for the Arts, and of SODEC.

Canada Council for the Arts Conseil des Arts du Canada

Société de développement des entreprises culturelles Québec

Railfare DC Books

Ontario office:
1880 Valley Farm Road, Unit #TP-27, Pickering, ON L1V 6B3

Business office and mailing address:
Box 666, St. Laurent Station, Montreal, QC H4L 4V9
email: railfare@videotron.ca web: www.railfare.net

CONTENTS

Note to Readers:

All railway and builder histories and checklists are found in the Premiere Volume of *Canadian National Steam!*, Section 2, pages 52-126. Explanations for technical and specification codes or abbreviations used in this volume are found in Section 9, General Notes for the Roster Project on pages 250-256.

X CLASS: 1-50

THIS SECTION

CNR 1-50 — X CLASS
MISCELLANEOUS TYPES

The "X" class was assigned road numbers **1-99** primarily for the narrow gauge locomotives of the former **Prince Edward Island Railway** and various dinkey and tank engines with various driver diameters. The class, totalling 44 locomotives, came from three predecessor roads: fifteen from **Grand Trunk Railway of Canada**; 28 from the **Canadian Government Railways**; and one from **Canadian Northern Railway** via the **Mount Royal Tunnel & Terminal Company Limited.**

In 1919 the road number allotment pattern assigned **1-2** and **10-35** to CGR (PEIR) locomotives; **3** to TT, and in 1923, **36-50** to those of the GTR. All dates are mm-dd-yr.

CNR 1 — 0-4-0T SADDLE TANK TYPE 3'6" — X-1-a

Specifications							Appliances		Weights	Fuel Capacity		Length	Notes
Cylinder	Gear	Driv.	Pressure	Boiler	T.E.	Haulage	Steam	Stkr.	Drivers/Eng./Total	Water	Coal		
8x16"	S	24"	150#	ST?	6000	6%	sat		30/ 30/ 000	gals	tons	- '	

Davenport Locomotive Works 1910 — (1) Acquired by CNR 9-01-1919

	Serial	Shipped	New as	7-03-1918	Disposition		To
1	—	-10	**DRMCo 1 ?**	**CGR (PEIR) 36**	So	4-01-30 AK	**Price 1**
-	—	-10	DRMCo 2 ?	(CGR (PEIR) 37)?	So	-23 AD?	AW&Co 1

CNR 1, in storage, possibly at Borden, PEI sometime during the early 1920s, had reacquired its former construction company number, although larger than an earlier one. Besides the CNR standard numeral format, a haulage rating and class were added. Although the use of an upper case letter for the sub-class would eventually be replaced in general practice with lower case letters, the style of "A" on the 0-4-0T's cab would never be altered. The missing coal pocket had probably been removed to facilitate the use of a tank tender during a earlier construction contract. [JAMES L. O'DONNELL COLLECTION]

CNR 1 was one of two locomotives built for the contractor **D.R. Morrison**, who may have used them in Newfoundland to construct the Anglo-Newfoundland Development Company's extension of the Millertown Railway to Harpoon Brook (the Harpoon Tramway). However, a check of Davenport records show no 0-4-0Ts built with 8x16 24 specifications nor **D.R. Morrison** as a customer. Both were transferred to PEI sometime in 1915 or 1916 when the firm D.R. Morrison & Son became one of the contractors involved in building the new railway termi-

(text continues on next page)

nal and ferry dock at Borden. With the completion of the work and the opening of the terminal on October 15th 1917, the construction equipment was put up for sale.

DRM 1, along with sixteen dump cars, was subsequently sold to the **Prince Edward Island** division of the **Canadian Government Railways** as **36**, although the sale was once thought to have included the second engine as 37. After 1919 DRM 1 became **CNR 1** and on the *CNR Mechanical Department Locomotive Diagrams* the 0-4-0T was identified as a "Dinkey Type".

It was sold for $600 to **Harold N. Price** of Moncton, New Brunswick, who planned to resell it as a stationary boiler to a local mill. He moved the 0-4-0T on a flat car from the Moncton scrap yard to the end of steel on CNR's wharf track, near the site of the former Moncton & Buctouche Railway station. It was unloaded next to a warehouse owned by Ambrose Wheeler and placed on rails laid between the standard gauge tracks. Remaining unsold, the derelict locomotive was finally sold and cut up by Isaac Gordon, a local scrap dealer. DRM 2(?) was likely never sold to the CGR-PEIR as 37, but instead remained in storage on the island. CNR documentation only mentions one saddle tank engine and the dump cars purchased in 1918. The second engine was finally sold in 1923 to Armstrong, Whitworth and Company, and may have been used with former CGR(PEIR) 219-220, 223-224 and 227 in the construction of the Howley Dam (near Corner Brook) before being scrapped at the end of the contract.

CNR 2 — 0-4-0 SWITCHER TYPE 4'8½" — X-2-a

Specifications							Appliances		Weights	Fuel Capacity		Length	Notes
Cylinder	Gear	Driv.	Pressure	Boiler	T.E.	Haulage	Steam	Stkr.	Drivers/Eng./Total	Water	Fuel		
17x24"	S	50"	150#	ST	17700	18%	sat		84/ 84/157000	2000 gals	5 tons	51-2½'	[CGR]

Pennsylvania Railroad Company – Altoona Machine Shop 1896 — (1) Acquired by CNR 9-01-1919

	Serial	Shipped	New as	-12?	8-1914	12-15-1915	Disposition
			—	—	—	S2	
2	1975	1-17-96	**PRR 638**	**NB&PEI 4**	**CGR 1177**	**CGR 1177**	Sc 7- -22 AK

CNR 2 was built as **Pennsylvania Railroad 638**, one of 84 U (A3) class 0-4-0s built by the road between 1895 and 1905. It was sold May 17, 1913 to **General Equipment Co.**, then to **Canadian Equipment Co.** before becoming **New Brunswick & Prince Edward Island Railway Company** No. 4 when construction began for the new Cape Traverse–Borden ferry terminal. When the NB&PEI was sold to the Government of Canada, the 0-4-0 was acquired by the **Canadian Government Railways** and classified the following year.

Even though the print of **CGR 1177** is disappointingly cropped, it is better than having none at all of the hand-me-down 0-4-0. The photograph is labelled as taken in Moncton during June 1922, and if so, it would appear the steamer was never relettered or renumbered to CNR livery, although it had been taken into stock in 1919. It was scrapped a month later, likely still wearing its PRR-style of builder's plate.
[JAMES L. O'DONNELL COLLECTION]

CNR 3 — 0-4-0T SADDLE TANK TYPE 3'6" — X-3-a

Cylinder	Gear	Driv.	Pressure	Boiler	T.E.	Haulage	Steam	Stkr.	Drivers/Eng./Total	Water	Coal	Length	Notes
14x22"	S	43"	180#	ST?	15000	15%	sat		58/ 58/ 000	gals	tons	- '	[CaNoR]
14x22"	S	43"	180#	ST?	15000	15%	sat		74/ 74/ 000	gals	tons	- '	

Rogers Locomotive Works - ALCO 1913 (J-1891) — (1) Acquired by CNR 9-01-1919

	Serial	Shipped	New as		1-1917?	Disposition	To
3	53867	7- -13	**MM&Co 11***	**(MRT&T) 11**	**CaNoR (ELD) 11**	So 4- -26 LN	**Acme**

Decorated as if it was a pride-of-the-fleet express locomotive of the 1870s, **MM&C 11** (CNR 3) had its builder's photograph taken at Paterson, New Jersey during July 1913. The extent of the trim and striping, particularly the wheel spokes and cylinder chest, might appear excessive, particularly when it was purchased for tunnel construction. The full length saddle tank extending from the firebox to the smokebox was somewhat unusual for this type of industrial switcher. [ROGERS WORKS PHOTO/ANDREW MERRILEES COLLECTION/ LIBRARY AND ARCHIVES CANADA PAC 207360]

CNR 3 was built in the first of three sets of twenty stock locomotives constructed near the end of locomotive production at the Rogers plant. It was ordered by and lettered **MacKenzie, Mann & Company** for the **Mount Royal Tunnel & Terminal Company Limited.** Although electric locomotives similar to those used in mines were used inside the tunnel, the steamer was probably used on the north end to carry away the spoil.

When tunnel construction was finished, the 0-4-0T was relocated (perhaps lettered **CaNoR 11**, but without a locomotive class) to **Canadian Northern Railway's Eastern Lands Division** tie plant opened in January 1917 at Foleyet, Ontario. It remained at this site during the CNR operation of the plant after 1919, but was sold for $2000 when the plant was purchased by **Acme Timber Company** in April 1926.

Acme Timber became **Pineland Timber Company** on March 15th 1934, but it is not known whether the switcher was still in service at this time. There is a possibility it was transferred to the Acme mill near Tionaga, Ontario before retirement. On *CNR Mechanical Department Locomotive Diagrams* the 0-4-0T was identified as a "Dinkey Type".

4-9 — **Numbers not used**

CNR 10-27 — 4-4-0 EIGHT-WHEEL TYPE 3'6" — X-4-a

CNR 10-27 were all built for the narrow gauge **Prince Edward Island Railway**. When the 4-4-0s were relettered **Canadian Government Railways**, all were assigned a haulage rating but no class.

In November 1923 five of the class, out-of-service at Charlottetown (**19-20**, **23-24** and **27**), were sold for $2500 each as construction locomotives to **Lamoreaux-Kelly Limited**, a Montreal contractor. They were reported as being used by this company during its contract to build the Newfoundland Power and Paper Company mill at Corner Brook (Bowater's Newfoundland Pulp & Paper Mills Limited after 1938). With the completion of the mill, the five 4-4-0s became **Armstrong, Whitworth & Company** 219-220, 223-224 and 227. They were used in the construction of the Main (Howley) Dam on Junction Brook near Corner Brook, before being scrapped at the end of the contract.

CNR 10 — 4-4-0 EIGHT-WHEEL TYPE 3'6" — X-4-a

The history for **10** is under CNR 18 (page X-8).

CNR 11-14 — 4-4-0 EIGHT-WHEEL TYPE 3'6" — X-4-a

Specifications							Appliances		Weights	Fuel Capacity		Length	Notes
Cylinder	Gear	Driv.	Pressure	Boiler	T.E.	Haulage	Steam	Stkr.	Drivers/Eng./Total	Water	Fuel		
14x18"	S	48"	139#	ST?	8000?	8%	sat		/ / 000	gals	tons	- '	[11-14]

Canadian Locomotive & Engine Company 1882 (C-6) — (4) Acquired by CNR 9-01-1919

	Serial	Shipped	New as	12-15-1915	Disposition
(11)	227	10-18-82	**PEIR 3/2**	**CGR (PEIR) 3**	Sc 9-30-20 AK
(12)	228	10-18-82	**PEIR 4/2***	**CGR (PEIR) 4**	Sc 9-30-20 AK
(13)	229	10-24-82	**PEIR 5/2**	**CGR (PEIR) 5**	Sc 9-30-20 AK
(14)	230	11-06-82	**PEIR 6/2**	**CGR (PEIR) 6**	Sc 9-30-20 AK

PEIR 3-6 (**11-14**) were in the third order from the Kingston builder placed by the **Prince Edward Island Railway** to replace four Hunslet-built 4-4-0Ts with the same road numbers which had been sold in 1881 to the Harbour Grace Railway in Newfoundland. Although assigned new numbers and a class, all were dismantled before any CNR livery was applied.

PEIR 4 (12) was posed dockside for its builder's photograph at Kingston in October 1882. The overexposure, obscuring some of the detail, was caused by the backlit view chosen by the photographer. He chose the view across the open water of the harbour to minimize distracting detail behind the image of the 4-4-0. [CL&ECO PHOTO/KENNETH S.MACDONALD COLLECTION]

CGR (PEIR) 3 (II) at Summerside on September 5th 1917 had undergone some upgrading since its delivery thirty-seven years previously. Besides moving the sand dome towards the rear of the boiler, the smokebox had been extended, although still not far enough forward to eliminate the need for a base to support a newer style of headlight. The high coalbox bunker had disappeared and the slatted pilot altered to function as a footboarded snow plow. [JOHN TINKLER PHOTO/SIRMAN COLLECTION]

CNR 15 & 21

4-4-0 EIGHT-WHEEL TYPE 3'6" **X-4-a**

Specifications							Appliances		Weights	Fuel Capacity		Length	Notes
Cylinder	Gear	Driv.	Pressure	Boiler	T.E.	Haulage	Steam	Stkr.	Drivers/Eng./Total	Water	Coal		
15x18"	S	69"	130#	ST?	8000?	8%	sat		/ / 000	gals	tons	- '	[15 new]
15x18"	S	54"	130#	ST?	8000?	8%	sat		/ / 000	gals	tons	- '	[15 rblt]
15x18"	S	62"	130#	ST?	9000?	9%	sat		/ / 000	gals	tons	- '	[21 new]
15x20"	S	48"	150#	ST?	11900?	12%	sat		45/ 70/ 000	gals	tons	- '	[21 rblt]

Canadian Locomotive & Engine Company 1884 (C-15) (2) Acquired by CNR 9-01-1919

	Serial	Shipped	New as	12-15-1915	Disposition
15/1	294	5-31-84	**PEIR 7**/3	**CGR (PEIR) 7**	Sc 2- -21 AK
21	295	5-31-84	**PEIR 21***	**CGR (PEIR) 21**	Sc 2- -21 A

PEIR 7 and 21 (15 and 21) were in a repeat order which continued the railway's preference for new locomotives to be constructed in Kingston. The builder supplied all the railway's needs for new power between 1876 and 1918, which would eventually total twenty-two 4-4-0 and eight 2-6-0 locomotives.

PEIR 21 (CNR 21) at the Kingston waterfront in May 1884, was photographed in the same location and in the same way as PEIR 4 (above) seventeen months earlier. However, there were some subtle differences between the two orders. PEIR 21 was built with a larger steam dome, a different style of driving wheel counterweights, and with spoked pilot wheels. The change in the style of tender lettering and numbering was perhaps the most obvious. [CL&ECO PHOTO/KENNETH S. MACDONALD COLLECTION]

CNR 16 & 20 — 4-4-0 EIGHT-WHEEL TYPE 3'6" — X-4-a

Cylinder	Gear	Driv.	Pressure	Boiler	T.E.	Haulage	Steam	Stkr.	Drivers/Eng./Total	Water	Fuel	Length	Notes
Specifications							Appliances		Weights	Fuel Capacity			
15x20"	S	48"	150#	ST	11000	12%	sat		45/ 70/102300	2250 gals	4 tons	46-1'	[16,20]

Canadian Locomotive & Engine Company 1899 — (2) Acquired by CNR 9-01-1919

	Serial	Shipped	New as	12-15-1915	Disposition	To	12-1924
16/1	470	7-29-99	**PEIR 8**	**CGR (PEIR) 16**	Sc 2- -23 AK		
20	471	7-29-99	**PEIR 20**	**CGR (PEIR) 20**	So11- -23 AD	**L-K 20**	**AW&Co 220**

X-4-a

PEIR 8 and 20 (**16** and **20**) were shipped on flat cars, arriving in Moncton on August 7th 1890 in transit to the island. They continued their journey on the IRC to Pictou, loaded on the steamer *HILLSBOROUGH*, and arrived in Charlottetown on August 18th 1899. Both were removed from the roster as the conversion to standard gauge between Royalty Jct. and Tignish was accomplished on August 11th 1923. See the general note under CNR 10-27 for the disposition of **20** (page X-5).

Even with a clerestory cab roof, PEIR 20 (CNR 20), at the Charlottetown wharf about 1905, had more the appearance of a twentieth century steamer than the 4-4-0s delivered to the island between 1882 and 1887. By the time of the photograph, large numbers had replaced the railway's initials on the side of the tender, although the pin-and-link coupling system had yet to be replaced. The metal sheathing covering the pilot slats was a common feature on many PEIR steamers, not only to clear the line of light snow, but also to prevent accumulated snow and ice from derailing the pilot trucks. [FRITZ LEHMANN COLLECTION]

CNR 17 — 4-4-0 EIGHT-WHEEL TYPE 3'6" — X-4-a

Cylinder	Gear	Driv.	Pressure	Boiler	T.E.	Haulage	Steam	Stkr.	Drivers/Eng./Total	Water	Fuel	Length	Notes
Specifications							Appliances		Weights	Fuel Capacity			
15x20"	S	48"	130#	ST?	10000?	10%	sat		/ / 000	gals	tons	- '	

Canadian Locomotive & Engine Company 1887 (C-20) — (1) Acquired by CNR 9-01-1919

	Serial	Shipped	New as	12-15-1915	Disposition
17/1	326	6- -87	**PEIR 10**/2	**CGR (PEIR) 10**	Sc 7- -23 AK

PEIR 10 (17) was recorded in service by June 23rd 1887. It was removed from service as the conversion to standard gauge between Royalty Jct. and Tignish was completed on August 11th 1923.

As the PEIR underwent standard gauging in the 1920s, all of the older power was removed from service. One of the earliest removals was **CNR 17**, believed to be on the Charlottetown wharf after its retirement in 1923, just before the gauge west of Borden was changed and the third rail removed in August 1923. Prior to the lifting of the rails, it and two others were shipped to Moncton for dismantling. CNR 17 was the first to be built with a cab clerestory roof, a PEIR practice which remained until 1904. [*CNR LOCOMOTIVE DATA CARD*]

CNR 10, 18-19, 26-27 — 4-4-0 EIGHT-WHEEL TYPE 3'6" — X-4-a

Specifications							Appliances		Weights	Fuel Capacity		Length	Notes
Cylinder	Gear	Driv.	Pressure	Boiler	T.E.	Haulage	Steam	Stkr.	Drivers/Eng./Total	Water	Coal		
15x20"	S	48"	130#	ST	8000?	8%	sat		/ 50/ 000	1800 gals	tons	- '	[10 new]
15x20"	S	54"	150#	ST	10900	11%	sat		45/ 70/126750	2200 gals	4 tons	47-4½'	[10 rblt; 18-19, 26-27]

Canadian Locomotive Company 1904 — (5) Acquired by CNR 9-01-1919

	Serial	Shipped	New as	by 11-1907	12-15-1915	Disposition	To	12-1924
10	616	4-30-04	**PEIR 1**/3		**CGR (PEIR) 1**	Sc 12- -24 AK		
18/1	617	4-23-04	**PEIR 11**/2		**CGR (PEIR) 11**	Sc 12- -24 A		
19	625	(4-19-04)	**PEIR 28**/1*	**PEIR 19**/2	**CGR (PEIR) 19**	So 11- -23 AD	**L-K 19**	**AW&Co 219**
26	618	4-30-04	**PEIR 26**		**CGR (PEIR) 26**	Sc 12- -24 AK		
27	619	5-04-04	**PEIR 27**		**CGR (PEIR) 27**	So 11- -23 AD	**L-K 27**	**AW&Co 227**

PEIR 1st **28** (19) was located for the company photographer on the transfer table at Kingston a few days before April 19th 1904, the day it was recorded shipped. The narrow gauge 4-4-0 was destined to travel further than most PEIR locomotives. Before entering service on what was to become its first island assignment, it had starred in the CLC's display at the 1904 World's Fair at St. Louis, Missouri. After twenty years on Prince Edward Island it moved to Newfoundland, working out its final assignments at Corner Brook. Although built with many turn-of-the-century appliances and design features, it still carried the trademark clerestory cab roof of an "Islander".
[CLC, HENDERSON PHOTO/QUEEN'S UNIVERSITY ARCHIVES]

PEIR 1, 11, 26 and 27 (**10**, **18**, **26** and **27**) were ordered in October 1903 and were on the Island by June 1904. PEIR first 28 (**19**) was shipped from CLC in April 1904 to the **World's Fair** held in **St. Louis**, Missouri as part of the Canadian Locomotive Company display. It was not delivered to the island railway until the fall of 1904. It was renumbered to second **19** sometime before 1907 either to fill the vacancy left by retired first 19 (0-4-4F CL&ECo 1880 #197?) or to avoid conflict with the new **PEIR 28** {#781}, which may have been numbered incorrectly by the builder.

All were removed from the roster after the conversion to standard gauge was completed between Royalty Jct. and Tignish on August 11th 1923. See the general note under CNR 10-27 for the disposition of **19** and **27** (page X-5).

CNR 15-18 (second)

See CNR Newfoundland Division list

CNR 20-21 — 4-4-0 EIGHT-WHEEL TYPE 3'6" — X-4-a

The history for **20** is under 16 (page X-7), the history for **21** is under 15 (page X-6).

CNR 22-23 — 4-4-0 EIGHT-WHEEL TYPE 3'6" — X-4-a

Cylinder	Gear	Driv.	Pressure	Boiler	T.E.	Haulage	Steam	Stkr.	Drivers/Eng./Total	Water	Fuel	Length	Notes
15x20"	S	48"	150#	ST	11000	12%	sat		45/ 70/102300	2250 gals	4 tons	46-1'	[22-23]

Canadian Locomotive & Engine Company 1900 — (2) Acquired by CNR 9-01-1919

	Serial	Shipped	New as	12-15-1915	Disposition	To	12-1924
22	496	9-29-00	**PEIR 22**	**CGR (PEIR) 22**	Sc 2- -23 AD		
23	497	9-29-00	**PEIR 23**	**CGR (PEIR) 23**	So11- -23 AD	**L-K 23**	**AW&Co 223**

PEIR 22 and 23 were built to the same specifications as PEIR 16 and 20 the year before. Both were removed from the roster during and after the conversion to standard gauge between Royalty Jct. and Tignish was completed on August 11th 1923. See the general note under CNR 10-27 for the disposition of **23** (page X-5).

CNR 24-25 — 4-4-0 EIGHT-WHEEL TYPE 3'6" — X-4-a

Cylinder	Gear	Driv.	Pressure	Boiler	T.E.	Haulage	Steam	Stkr.	Drivers/Eng./Total	Water	Fuel	Length	Notes
15x20"	S	54"	150#	ST	9910	11%	sat		45/ 70/127250	2250 gals	4 tons	46-4'	[24-25]

Canadian Locomotive Company 1901 — (2) Acquired by CNR 9-01-1919

	Serial	Shipped	New as	12-15-1915	Disposition	To	12-1924
24	520	12-17-01	**PEIR 24**	**CGR (PEIR) 24**	So11- -23 AD	**L-K 24**	**AW&Co 224**
25	521	12-26-01	**PEIR 25**	**CGR (PEIR) 25**	Sc 7- -23 AK		

PEIR 24 and 25 were shipped from Kingston to Pictou on CPR flat cars, loaded onto scows, and towed across the Northumberland Strait to Charlottetown. Both were removed from the roster during and after the conversion to standard gauge between Royalty Jct. and Tignish was achieved on August 11th 1923. See the general note under CNR 10-27 for the disposition of **24** (page X-5).

CNR 26-27 — 4-4-0 EIGHT-WHEEL TYPE 3'6" — X-4-a

The history for **26-27** is under 10 (see page X-8).

CNR 28-31 — 4-6-0 TEN-WHEEL TYPE 3'6" — X-5-a

Specifications							Appliances		Weights	Fuel Capacity		Length	Notes
Cylinder	Gear	Driv.	Pressure	Boiler	T.E.	Haulage	Steam	Stkr.	Drivers/Eng./Total	Water	Coal		
16½x22"	S	57"	175#	ST	15600	16%	sat		74/ 95/162900	3000 gals	4 tons	43-6'	

Canadian Locomotive Company 1907 $9000 — (4) Acquired by CNR 9-01-1919

	Serial	Shipped	New as	12-15-1915	Disposition
28	781	11-27-07	**PEIR 28/2***	**CGR (PEIR) 28**	Sc 5-31-27 AK
29	782	11-27-07	**PEIR 29**	**CGR (PEIR) 29**	Sc 5-31-27 AK
30	783	12-05-07	**PEIR 30**	**CGR (PEIR) 30**	Sc 5-31-27 AK
31	784	12-05-07	**PEIR 31**	**CGR (PEIR) 31**	Sc 5-31-27 AK

The last order for the PEIR consisted of four Ten Wheelers, which were to become the largest power on the railway. **PEIR** 2nd **28** (28), on the transfer table at Kingston in late November 1907, had an all-steel open cab with single side windows and small cab skirts, but no clerestory on the cab roof or turbo-generator for locomotive lighting. The simplified livery did not include the railway's name. [CLC, HENDERSON PHOTO/QUEEN'S UNIVERSITY ARCHIVES]

PEIR 28-31 were ordered by the **Prince Edward Island Railway** in two increments. The first pair was ordered in August 1906, and the second soon afterwards. The road number for **PEIR 28** was the second time it was used. It was either applied in error by the builder, or reused by the railway when the first 28 was renumbered to fill the vacancy left by the retirement of first 19.

When the four were relettered **Canadian Government Railways**, they were assigned a haulage rating but no class. All the 4-4-0s were removed from the roster either during or after the conversion of the line to standard gauge east of Royalty Jct. to Georgetown and to Elmira on August 22nd and 30th 1926 respectively.

CNR 32-35 — 4-6-0 TEN-WHEEL TYPE 3'6" — X-5-b

Specifications							Appliances		Weights	Fuel Capacity		Length	Notes
Cylinder	Gear	Driv.	Pressure	Boiler	T.E.	Haulage	Steam	Stkr.	Drivers/Eng./Total	Water	Coal		
16½x22"	W	57"	175#	EWT	15600	16%	SCH		77/100/171300	3000 gals	4 tons	51-7'	

Canadian Locomotive Company Limited 1918 (C-527) $34,571 — (4) Acquired by CNR 9-01-1919

	Serial	Shipped	Delivered	New as	Disposition
32	1521	8-22-18	9-13-18	**CGR (PEIR) 32**	Rs 12-31-30 AD Sc 12-22-32 AK
33	1522	8-29-18	9-13-18	**CGR (PEIR) 33**	Rs 12-31-30 AD Sc 12-22-32 AK
34	1523	9-28-18	10-02-18	**CGR (PEIR) 34***	Rs 12-31-30 AD Sc 12-22-32 AK
35	1524	9-28-18	10-02-18	**CGR (PEIR) 35**	Rs 12-31-30 AD Sc 12-22-32 AK

PEIR/CGR 32-35, ordered in January 1918 for the **Prince Edward Island Railway**, were lettered **Canadian Government Railways** on the cab when delivered from Kingston. The dates shown under "Delivered" (above) are considered to be the arrival or in-service dates on the Island. They carried a CGR haulage rating but no class.

CNR 34, powering the last narrow gauge, was run on September 27th 1930 between Murray Harbour and Charlottetown. They were removed from service on the date used above, although Issue B of the X-5-b *CNR Mechanical Department Locomotive Diagrams* show all four were "Removed From Records, Mar'31". All went to scrap without being converted to standard gauge.

The Canadian Locomotive Company, by far the preferred builder of PEIR steam power, built the last group for use on the island, even though it was operated by the CGR. **CGR 34** (34) at Kingston in September 1918 was delivered similar in design to the previous 4-6-0s, except for being superheated, equipped with a turbo-generator, and a full open steel cab. Altered markings included the Government road's name on the side of the cab. [CLC, BUTLER PHOTO C-537/ QUEEN'S UNIVERSITY ARCHIVES/DON MCQUEEN COLLECTION]

CNR 36 — 0-4-0T PANNIER SADDLE TANK TYPE — X-6-a

Cylinder	Gear	Driv.	Pressure	Boiler	T.E.	Haulage	Appliances: Steam	Stkr.	Weights: Drivers/Eng./Total	Fuel Capacity: Water	Fuel	Length	Notes
14x24"	S	44"	#	ST	00		sat		/ / 000	gals	wood	25-9'?	[orig 0-4-0T]
14x24"	S	44"	130#	ST	00		sat		48/ 40/ 57000	1245 gals	2½ tons	25-9'	[rblt GWR 0-4-2T after 1874]
14x24"	S	45"	130#	ST	11551	12%	sat		51/ 51/ 51000	1245 gals	2½ tons	25-9'	[rblt GTR 0-4-0T btwn 6-01 & 05]

M.W. Baldwin & Company 1872 — (1) Acquired by CNR 3-01-1923

	Serial	Shipped	New as	af. 1874	1882	1898	1902?	1902	To	1-1910	Disposition	To
			0-4-0T	0-4-2T	0-4-2T	0-4-2T	0-4-0T	0-4-2T				
			—	—	—	—	—	—	F8	F8		
—	2941	10- -72	GWR 308	GWR 408	GTR 903						So 6- -97	??
36	2943	10- -72	**GWR 309**	**GWR 409**	**GTR 904**	**GTR 610**	**GTR 7**		11-04	**GTR 2543**	So 7- -23 HQ	**Knox**
—	2953	11- -72	GWR 310	GWR 410	GTR 905	GTR 611		GTR 8	11-04	GTR 2541	So 5- -12	McG
—	2954	11- -72	GWR 311	GWR 411	GTR 906	GTR 612		GTR 9	11-04	GTR 2542	So 5- -12	McG
—	2959	11- -72	GWR 312	GWR 412	GTR 907						So 6- -97	??
—	2961	11- -72	GWR 313	GWR 413	GTR 908						So 6- -97	??

CNR 36 was one in an order of six standard gauge 0-4-0 wood-burning switchers built for the **Great Western Railway of Canada**, although the Baldwin records have them listed as 0-4-0T types. The identity of the original road numbers cannot be confirmed, and the numbers 308-313/408-413 are speculative. The build-date for GWR 309 (**36**) is given as September 1872. Sometime after 1874 GWR rebuilt the group into coal-burning 0-4-2T locomotives and may have renumbered them at that time. After amalgamation, they became **Grand Trunk Railway of Canada** switchers, with only GTR 6 and 7 (**37** and **36**) were rebuilt again as 0-4-0T types, sometime between June 1901 and June 1905 – perhaps in 1902 when they were renumbered.

Three of the 0-4-2Ts were sold in 1897 to an unidentified buyer. In 1912 two went to F.H. McGuigan Construction Company, thus leaving only the two 0-4-0Ts becoming CNR locomotives. The 0-4-0Ts were referred to as "Dinkey Type" in the *CNR Mechanical Department Locomotive Diagrams*. **CNR 36** was sold to **Knox Brothers**, a dealer or contractor from Montreal. The disposition of the other is unknown, although it might have been resold to the Harbour Commissioners of Montreal (see CNR 37 below).

CNR 37 — 0-4-0T PANNIER SADDLE TANK TYPE — X-6-a

Cylinder	Gear	Driv.	Pressure	Boiler	T.E.	Haulage	Appliances: Steam	Stkr.	Weights: Drivers/Eng./Total	Fuel Capacity: Water	Fuel	Length	Notes
14x24"	S	44"	#	ST	00		sat		/ / 000	gals	wood	- '	[see CNR 36]

M.W. Baldwin & Company 1873 $5300 — (1) Acquired by CNR 3-01-1923

	Serial	Shipped	New as	af. 1874	1882	1898	1902?	To	1-1910	Disposition	To
			0-4-0T	0-4-2T	0-4-2T	0-4-2T	0-4-0T	0-4-0T	0-4-0T		
			—	—	—	—	—	F8	F8		
—	3349	8- -73	GWR 418	GWR 396	GTR 897					So 5- -97	??
—	3353	8- -73	GWR 419	GWR 397	GTR 898					So 5- -97	MJH
—	3358	8- -73	GWR 420	GWR 398	GTR 899					So 9- -97	AO
37	3374	8- -73	**GWR** (321) or **421**	**GWR 399**	**GTR 900**	**GTR 609**	**GTR 6**	11-04	**GTR 2544**	So 2- -25 MHC	**LDL**

CNR 37 was one of another four standard gauge 0-4-0 wood-burning switchers built for the **Great Western Railway of Canada**, although the Baldwin records again have them listed as 0-4-0T types. The original GWR road numbers are open to speculation. The Baldwin register and order books show GWR 421 (**37**) ordered as GWR 321 but it was delivered as GWR 421. Sometime after 1874 GWR rebuilt the group into coal-burning 0-4-2T types and may have renumbered them at the same time. After amalgamation, they became **Grand Trunk Railway of Canada** switchers. Only GTR 6 and 7 (**37** and **36**) were rebuilt again as 0-4-0T types, sometime between June 1901 and June 1905 – perhaps in 1902 when they were renumbered.

Three of the 0-4-2Ts were sold in 1897, one to an unknown buyer, another to M.J. Hogan, and a third to Andrew Onderdonk. Only the two rebuilt 0-4-0Ts became CNR locomotives and, on the *CNR Mechanical Department Locomotive Diagrams*, referred to as "Dinkey Type". **CNR 37** was sold to **Lucien Dussault Limited** of Giffard, Quebec for $1000. It was likely 37 (and not CNR 36) which eventually became **Harbour Commissioners of Montreal** 11, as the former was sold to Dussault as is from the Harbour Commission's yard. HCM 11 was scrapped in May 1935.

CNR 38-40 — 0-4-0 SWITCHER TYPE — X-7-a

Specifications							Appliances		Weights	Fuel Capacity		Length	Notes
Cylinder	Gear	Driv.	Pressure	Boiler	T.E.	Haulage	Steam	Stkr.	Drivers/Eng./Total	Water	Coal		
16x24"	S	51"	180#	ST	18000?		sat		80/ 80/140000	2500 gals	5 tons sb	50-7'	[orig]
16x24"	S	51"	170#	ST	17408	17%	sat		80/ 80/140000	2500 gals	5 tons sb	50-7'	

Baldwin Locomotive Works – Burnham, Parry, Williams & Company 1898 $8000 (3) Acquired by CNR 3-01-1923

	Serial	Shipped	New as	1-1905	1-1910	Disposition	To
			B	F6	F6		
38	16095	7- -98	**CAR 3**	**GTR 1313**	**GTR 2555**	Sc 8- -25 HQ	
39	16096	7- -98	**CAR 4**	**GTR 1314**	**GTR 2556**	Sc 8- -25 HQ	
(40)	16097	7- -98	**CAR 5**	**GTR 1315**	**GTR 2557**	So 2- -24 C	**CWP**

Tender 0-4-0 switchers were rarely found in the rosters of CNR's predecessors. If the wheel arrangement was used at all, it was usually as a tank engine. Many of the tank switchers were rebuilds from 4-4-0s. A pair was recorded working on the N&NW in the 1880s, and at least one GTR tank was again modified to a tender switcher. Five, however, were built as 0-4-0 switchers. Two were used by the C&GT between 1882 and 1911. CAR acquired a trio from Baldwin in 1898 which eventually became part of the CNR roster. **GTR 1314**, on former CAR trackage in Ottawa prior to 1910, was to become CNR 39 and carry the number for about a year. [AL PATERSON COLLECTION]

CNR 38-40 were ordered by the **Canada Atlantic Railway**. *CNR Mechanical Department Locomotive Diagrams* for the X-7-a class showed the switchers with a slope-back tender, and had a out-of-service note "Removed Dec. 1924".

CNR 40 was sold to the **Continental Wood Products Company** as **GTR 2557** for $1800 and was known to have worked at the company mill at Foleyet, Ontario.

(text continues on next page)

CWP also had a mill at Elsas, Ontario between 1924 and 1929 but it is unclear whether or not the 0-4-0 was ever at this location. The 0-4-0 later became **Chambers, McQuigge & McCaffrey** 2557 where it was thought to have been used during 1928 and 1929 in the construction of the harbour and docks for the paper mill at Ware Point, Port Arthur, Ontario. Its final disposition is not known.

CNR "40" — 4-4-0 EIGHT-WHEEL TYPE 3'6" — -none-

Specifications							Appliances		Weights	Fuel Capacity		Length	Notes
Cylinder	Gear	Driv.	Pressure	Boiler	T.E.	Haulage	Steam	Stkr.	Drivers/Eng./Total	Water	Fuel		
16x24"	S	66"	#	ST	00		sat		80/ / 000	gals	tons	- '	[orig]

The Portland Company 1872 — (1) Acquired by CNR 1949

	Serial	Shipped	New as	1898	12-1902	1-1903	1949	Disposition	To
—	231	11- -72	GTR 360	GTR 125				Sc 11- -01	
—	232	11- -72	GTR 361	GTR 27				So 9- -01	SSR
"40"	233	11- -72	**GTR 362**	**GTR 40**	**GTR 129/2**	**CVRY 40**	**"CNR 40"**	Dn 6-16-67 C	**NMST**
—	234	11- -72	GTR 363	GTR 41				So 7- -01	SSR

The 4-4-0 photographed without the prescribed protective snow fence was on display with the Museum Train at an unidentified location. It was likely during 1954, soon after the removal of the zero prefix in the road number painted on the headlight lens. [SIRMAN COLLECTION]

CNR "40" was one of four standard gauge 4-4-0s built in 1872 for the **Grand Trunk Railway of Canada**. One was scrapped and a pair sold to the South Shore Railway Company of Quebec. The last one remaining in service was sold, as **GTR** second **129**, to the **John Breakey Lumber Company Limited** and relettered **Chaudiere Valley** 40.

It was acquired in 1949 and by 1950 restored sufficiently to be displayed for special events. One of the earliest was in St. Albans on October 18th 1950, to celebrate the centennial of the first trains to run on the CVR. Then it was moved to Michigan to be part of a July 4th 1951 celebration which commemorated Durand becoming a railway crossing town 75 years before. On August 1st 1951, The Canadian Locomotive Company feted a "Diesel Day" in Kingston to unveil their new Fairbanks-Morse line of road diesels, the "C-Liners". Both "40" and CLC-built pioneer Beardmore yard switcher 77 (#1861 12-1929) were part of the festivities beside the stars of the show, CLC CPA16-4 *CITY OF KINGSTON* 7005 and 7006 (later CPR 4064 and 4065). Number "40" again visited Vermont for a celebration on October 6th 1951, commemorating Northfield University's graduation of General Dodge a century before. During its 1950 and 1951 visits to Vermont and Michigan, the lettering on the tender was "Canadian National" and "Grand Trunk Western" respectively.

In 1952 Number "40" became the show piece for CNR's **Museum Train**. Its restoration was cosmetic rather than operational, although it did permit it to be towed at slow speed from place to place for exhibit. At least once, oily cotton waste was stuffed into the balloon stack and lit, producing smoke for photographic effect. (See Vol. 1, p. 157). It was first identified as a CNR locomotive by tender lettering and later with a tilted wafer. During its USA (Michigan and Vermont) visits, the lettering was altered to "Grand Trunk Western" on the tender. The number "40" was chosen to reflect its heritage both to its earlier GTR road number and that used by the CVRY. Initially the

(text continues on next page)

CNR "found" Chaudiere Valley 40 sitting idle after years of service on the Quebec short line. When its antiquity was traced, the company deemed it historically significant as a representative of the wood burning era and eventually suitable for inclusion in the Museum Train. There were some technical difficulties, however, of reconciling the reconstructed pointed "cow-catcher" of pin-and-link days with travel in the era of knuckle couplers. The earliest solution was a draw bar inserted into the coupler pocket, but later the wooden pilot was hinged to allow it to be raised and a standard knuckle coupler utilized. The latter was visible when 40 was donated to the NMST in Ottawa during June 1967. [DON McQUEEN COLLECTION]

road number painted on the headlight lens was "**040**", but later changed to "**40**".

After the retirement of the CNR Museum Train in 1958, the 4-4-0 continued to be used occasionally for special events, one of the last being for the Haliburton railway centennial in 1964. It remained as part of the CNR Historical Collection until June 16th 1967 when it was donated, along with most of the Museum Train equipment, to the **National Museum of Science & Technology** (now the Canada Science & Technology Museum) in Ottawa, Ontario. It is ironic that both "40" and CPR 4065 (from the CLC "Diesel Day") currently reside at the CSTM.

CNR "40" is included in this roster not only because it is the only extant locomotive previously owned by the **Grand Trunk Railway of Canada** that was not acquired by the Canadian National Railways, but also as it is the only remaining Portland-built locomotive in existence. The plaque mounted on the engine during its travels also stated "it was the first locomotive built for the GTR after it converted its track from broad gauge (5'6") to the standard gauge (4'8½")."

CNR 41 — 4-4-2ST SIDE TANK SUBURBAN TYPE — X-8-a

Specifications							Appliances		Weights	Fuel Capacity		Length	Notes
Cylinder	Gear	Driv.	Pressure	Boiler	T.E.	Haulage	Steam	Stkr.	Drivers/Eng./Total	Water	Coal		
17x22"	S	63"	140#	ST	12009	12%	sat		75/134/134200	1530 gals	3 tons	38-9'	

Grand Trunk Railway – Pointe St.Charles 1883 $10,000 — (1) Acquired by CNR 3-01-1923

	Serial	Shipped	New as	1898	11-1904	1-1910	Mods	Disposition
			—	—	K1	K1		
41	1121	5- -83	**GTR 191**	**GTR 267**	**GTR 202**	**GTR 1527**	p	Sc 10-13-23 HQ

CNR 41 was one of ten built between May and August 1883 by **Grand Trunk Railway of Canada** as 190-199. Five in the order were rebuilt into 4-4-0 types in 1888. See the entry under CNR 4-4-0 126 for the complete history of the order (page A-10).

GTR 1527 (41) at Turcot before 1919 was in the first lot of side tank engines built by GTR specifically for Montreal's suburban trains. The first pair had been converted from 4-4-0s. In a reverse process, five from this group were rebuilt and survived long enough to become CNR A-9-a 4-4-0s. By the time of the photograph, the coal bunker had been rebuilt, and the cab remodelled and steel plated. An electric headlight was not installed until September 1919. [CNR PHOTO 37014/CANADA SCIENCE & TECHNOLOGY MUSEUM COLLECTION](W.D. (BILL) THOMSON)

CNR 42-44 — 4-4-2ST SIDE TANK SUBURBAN TYPE — X-9-a

Specifications							Appliances		Weights	Fuel Capacity		Length	Notes
Cylinder	Gear	Driv.	Pressure	Boiler	T.E.	Haulage	Steam	Stkr.	Drivers/Eng./Total	Water	Fuel		
17x22"	S	63"	150#	ST	12867	13%	sat		69/129/129000	1530 gals	3 tons	40-6'	
17x22"	S	63"	160#	ST	14000		sat		88/158/158246	gals	3 tons	40-5'	[4-4-2PT; GTR 275]

Grand Trunk Railway – Pointe St. Charles 1892 $10,000 (3) Acquired by CNR 3-01-1923

	Serial	Shipped	New as	1898	11-1904	1-1910	Leased TIR	Mods	Disposition	To
			—	—	K1	K1				
42	1249	2- -92	**GTR-TBLR 39***	**GTR 271**	**GTR 206**	**GTR 1531**	1923-1924	p	Sc 3-05-25 LM	
43	1250	2- -92	**GTR-TBLR 40**	**GTR 272**	**GTR 207**	**GTR 1532**	1924-1934	p	Sc 9-28-34 HQ	
44	1251	2- -92	**GTR-TBLR 41**	**GTR 273**	**GTR 208**	**GTR 1533**		p	So 12-16-27 HQ	**TIR 44**
—	1252	3- -92	GTR-TBLR 42	GTR 274	GTR 209	GTR 1534		p	Sc 9- -14	
—	1253	3- -92	GTR-TBLR 43	GTR 275	GTR 210	GTR 1535		p	Sc 7- -16	

In 1892 GTR built its second batch of suburban side-tanks for Belt Line trains in Toronto. **GTR 39** (42) was thought to be photographed in Toronto between 1892 and 1894 before its transfer to Montreal. [AL PATERSON COLLECTION]

GTR 275 as a Pannier saddle tank engine, at an unidentified location in Montreal between 1898 and 1904, had a tank which had been lengthened and raised to clear the drivers. Although being described as a switcher, it had road engine front and rear pilots rather than footboards.
[AL PATERSON COLLECTION]

GTR 1534, in Montreal between 1910 and 1914, was in sharp contrast in appearance when compared with the as-built 39. Besides the change in headlight, the remodelled cab had been steel-plated with square-cornered windows and the coal bunker enlarged.
[AL PATERSON COLLECTION]

CNR 42-44 were part of an order for five built by the **Grand Trunk Railway of Canada** for use on the **Toronto Belt Line Railway** beginning in 1892. When service ended in 1894, these "Belt Line Tanks", as they were known, were transferred to Montreal suburban service. Sometime between 1898 and 1904, **GTR 275** was rebuilt into a 4-4-2PT – a Pannier Tank switcher. This differed from side tank engines in that the tanks were attached to the boiler rather than to the running plates.

GTR disposed of two in the lot before 1923. **CNR 42** was leased by the **Thousand Islands Railway** between

(text continues on next page)

1923 and 1924 (replacing GTR 2049) and was returned as a result of damage in a 1924 accident, although details of the incident are incomplete. It was replaced by 43 which remained leased until 1934. **CNR 44** was sold to the **Thousand Islands Railway**, and lettered **TIR 44** to replace the retired **TIR(CNR) 241**. Base cost was $3000 plus $3700 worth of repairs. With the arrival of TIR's gas electric number 500 in March 1931, **TIR 44** became the spare locomotive until it was retired in 1934. It remained in the TIR engine house until it was scrapped in 1937.

Belt Line Suburbans which worked assignments beyond Toronto and Montreal included a trio which saw service on the TIR. **CNR 43** at the Gananoque riverfront station had replaced its mate, number 42 in 1924. The CNR wafer, applied sometime after late 1927, was retained as the 4-4-2ST was only leased to the TIR. [SIRMAN COLLECTION]

Purchased and lettered, **TIR 44** (CNR 44) was about to leave from the Gananoque waterfront for the Junction in June 1930. Other than the sectional cab windows, turbo-generators, and triangular road number lamp, the Suburbans were relatively unaltered from their days in GTR service. The water tank's filling saddle was visible nestled between the sand and steam domes. [HAROLD K. VOLLRATH/WES DENGATE COLLECTION]

CNR 45-50 — 4-6-2FT SUBURBAN TYPE — X-10-a

Specifications							Appliances		Weights	Fuel Capacity		Length	Notes
Cylinder	Gear	Driv.	Pressure	Boiler	T.E.	Haulage	Steam	Stkr.	Drivers/Eng./Total	Water	Fuel		
31x26"	W	63"	210#	ST	32487	32%	SCH		146/146/275000	2900 gals	5 tons	50-2'	[CNR]

Montreal Locomotive Works Limited - ALCO 1914 (Q-241) $18,229 — (6) Acquired by CNR 3-01-1923

	Serial	Shipped	New as	— E-fwh —		Mods	Disposition	To
			K2	GTR	CNR			
45	54894	9- -14	**GTR 1540**	1-28 HQ		pm	Sc 8-24-56 HQ	
46	54895	9- -14	**GTR 1541**		2-25 HQ	pm	So 7-26-61 HQ	**VSHS**
47	54896	9- -14	**GTR 1542**		7-26 HQ	pmr	So 6-15-59 HQ	**STM**
48	54897	9- -14	**GTR 1543**	6-22 HQ		pm z	Sc 1-30-59 LM	
49	54898	9- -14	**GTR 1544**		1-28 HQ	pmr	So 9-15-60 HQ	**CRHA**
50	54899	9- -14	**GTR 1545**	1-22 HQ		pmr	Sc 4-07-60 LM	

Fresh from the builder, **GTR 1540** (45), at Pointe St. Charles in September 1914, would eventually be outfitted with an electric headlight in May 1917 and improved handrail locations in August 1918, five years before the installation of the feedwater heater. [CNR PHOTO 37016/W.D. (BILL) THOMSON COLLECTION]

In addition to the installation of its feedwater heater at Pointe St. Charles in 1925, **46** had undergone other modifications. Besides the alteration of the smokebox front to CNR standards, front and rear boiler tube pilots installed, the cab's forward side windows blanked, the coal bunker had been extended and the bunker headlight relocated to the water deck. The alterations made to cab and bunker handrails in December 1920 can be seen when compared to those of GTR 1540. [CNR PHOTO 28878/AL PATERSON COLLECTION]

CNR 45-50 were built for the **Grand Trunk Railway of Canada** and came superheated with steel vestibule cabs from the builder, but acquired Elesco feedwater heaters during the 1920s. They were designed to haul seven-car suburban Montreal trains on the 24-mile run between the city and Vaudreuil and the 37-mile line to St. Hyacinthe.

All but one remained in Montreal commuter service until their retirement. Between 1955 and the end of its service life, **48** was assigned on two occasions to local trains outside the Montreal area. In August 1955 it was transferred to Allandale, but no recorded runs were made by the 4-6-4FT to supplant the area's self-propelled cars

(text continues on next page)

Minor improvements continued during the 1930s. CNR 50 at St. Henri station in Montreal in 1934 had already been equipped in January with a Hancock non-lifting inspirator which had been tucked in under the cab ahead of the ladder. A feedwater heater shield had been installed along the bottom of the Elesco bundle as well as a different model of bell ringer. [AL PATERSON COLLECTION]

which regularly ran between Hamilton and Allandale on trains 660/661 and 662/663. In March 1956 its second move was to Sarnia for trains 606-621 and 620-605, the Sarnia–London–Sarnia locals. It was stored in Sarnia in February 1957 and was returned to Turcot in October 1957 to replace 50 in commuter service. It remained in Montreal until August 1958 until it again returned to London in December 1958, this time for scrapping.

CNR 46 was bought in 1961 by **H. J. O'Connell** of Dorval, Quebec (under the name **H. J. O'Connell Supplies Limited**) who donated it in 1967 to the **Vaudreuil-Soulanges Historical Society** for eventual display. During that time it was stored in the O'Connell construction yard. When the project could not be accomplished, the locomotive was acquired in April 1969 by **Canadian Steel Products Limited**, who placed it on display in its Industrial Park in Longueil, Quebec. The company underwent a name change to **Quebec Steel Products** [SIDBEC]. In early August 2002 the 4-6-4FT was moved to **Le Centre d'Interpretation Ferroviaire de Vallée-Jonction** [CIF] at Vallée Jct., Quebec.

CNR 47, purchased for $2000 by **F. Nelson Blount** for his **Edaville Railroad Association**, was subsequently displayed at **Steamtown** in North Walpole, New Hampshire, and after 1984, in Scranton, Pennsylvania.

CNR 49, the last steam locomotive to be overhauled at Pointe St. Charles shops on August 23rd 1957, was sold for $3675 to the **Canadian Railroad Historical Association** for the **Canadian Railway Museum** at St. Constant, Quebec.

The running board on the fireman's side of 50, at Turcot on August 27th 1936, was a jungle of pumps. Above the first driver was the 8½-inch cross-compound air pump installed in September 1922. The water pumps with two separate simple cylinders and the piping connected to the feedwater heater were above the main driver. [DAVE SHAW/WES DENGATE COLLECTION]

Further changes took place during last two decades of service. **CNR 48**, at London's York Street station in 1957, had not only been fitted with full running board ladders, an upgraded Elesco feedwater pump, and cab skirts in the mid-1940s, but also a forked main crankpin connection. Raised cab numerals had been applied to all six 4-6-4FTs after 1950. The horizontal wafer was applied only to 48, although three others were shopped with the maple leaf roundel (r). [ROBERT (BOB) RAM PHOTO/DON McQUEEN COLLECTION]
A tender view of 46 in Montreal Lakeshore commuter service can be found in Vol. 1, p. 121.

This head-on view of X-10-a Suburban Type **CNR 50** at Pointe St. Charles shops in 1949, confirmed the notion a uniform standard of appearance was maintained by the company, even though physical dimensions of its locomotives varied. What might be a hint to the size of CNR 50 was the use of, and spacing of the two digits on the red-fielded brass road number plate, rather than the three or four digits used for larger power. [CNR PHOTO]

51-79	**Numbers not used**
CNR 80-96	(17) See CNR **902-926** E-10-a class (page E-51)
97-99	**Numbers not used**

CONTENTS

A CLASS: 100-172

THIS SECTION

CNR 100-172 — A CLASS
4-4-0 EIGHT-WHEEL TYPE

Class "A" was assigned road numbers **100-199** for American (Standard) or Eight-Wheel Types with drivers 63 inches or less. The class, totalling 74 locomotives, came from three predecessor roads; 47 from the **Grand Trunk Railway of Canada** (31 of which were assigned GTW lines); 14 from the **Canadian Northern Railway;** and 13 from the **Canadian Government Railway.**

In 1919 the road number allotment assigned **100-102** and **116-127** to CaNoR 4-4-0s and **104-115** to those of the CGR. In 1923 the GTR-GTW 4-4-0s were assigned the numbers **126-172.**

Although the distribution of the A class sub-series assigned by the CNR Motive Power Department in 1919 may appear to be lacking sequential order, it should be noted the class was built around CaNoR classes still in use. CaNoR vacancies were reused to classify CGR and GTR motive power both in 1919 and 1923 respectively. The practice continued for other stock acquired after 1924. These reassigned CaNoR classes are listed in Part Two: *CNR Class Summary*. All dates are mm-dd-yr.

CNR 100-102 — 4-4-0 EIGHT-WHEEL TYPE — A-1-a

Specifications							Appliances		Weights	Fuel Capacity		Length	Notes
Cylinder	Gear	Driv.	Pressure	Boiler	T.E.	Haulage	Steam	Stkr.	Drivers/Eng./Total	Water	Coal		
17x24"	S	62"	140#	EWT	13313		sat		62/ 96/181000	4000 gals	10 tons	54-8'	[100 CaNoR 1909]
17x24"	S	62"	150#	EWT	14263		sat		62/ 96/181000	4000 gals	10 tons	54-8'	[100 CaNoR 1909]
17x24"	S	63"	150#	EWT	14100	14%	sat		62/ 96/181000	4000 gals	10 tons	54-8'	[100-101]
17x24"	S	63"	140#	EWT	13160	13%	sat		62/ 96/162000	2500 gals	8 tons	54-4'	[102]

Canadian Locomotive & Engine Company (Dübs) 1895; 1896 — (3) Acquired by CNR 9-01-1919

	Serial	Shipped	New as	1899	1-1912	Disposition
			—	—	A-1-A 14%	
(100)	454	10-13-96	**LMR&C 2**	**CaNoR 2**	**CaNoR 2**	Sc 12-08-20 PK
(101)	455	10-27-96	**LMR&C 3**	**CaNoR 3**	**CaNoR 3**	Sc 7-12-20 PK
(102)	449	6-19-95	**IB&O 2**	—	**(CaNoR) IB&O 4**	Sc 7- -22 MU

CNR **100** and **101** were built for the **Lake Manitoba Railway and Canal Company** before the company was reorganized as the **Canadian Northern Railway** by MacKenzie and Mann in 1899.

102 was ordered as a single locomotive by the **Irondale Bancroft & Ottawa Railway.**

103 — Road number and class not used — A-2-a

CNR 104 — 4-4-0 EIGHT-WHEEL TYPE — A-3-a

Specifications							Appliances		Weights	Fuel Capacity		Length	Notes
Cylinder	Gear	Driv.	Pressure	Boiler	T.E.	Haulage	Steam	Stkr.	Drivers/Eng./Total	Water	Coal		
18x24"	S	60"	160#		16000		sat		/ 94/ 000	gals	tons	- '	[orig]
18x24"	S	63"	150#		16000		sat		/ 97/ 000	gals	tons	- '	[bf. 10-1914]
18x24"	S	62"	160#	EWT	17000	17%	sat		62/ 97/169000	2700 gals	6 tons	51-5'	[CGR, CNR]

Dübs & Company 1888 — (1) Acquired by CNR 9-01-1919

	Serial	Shipped	New as	1910	1-04-1912	12-1915	1917	Retired	Disposition	To
			—		D13 171%	A2-13 85%				
104	2359	7- -88	**IRC 33/3***		**IRC 1027**	**CGR 1027**			Sc 10- -22	
—	2360	7- -88	IRC 146/2		IRC 1031			bf. 10- -14	Ss -17	CC&F
—	2361	7- -88	IRC 160/2	Ls C&F	IRC 1030	CGR 1030	Ls IR&C	12-18-17	Sc -18	

CNR 104 was in a group of three 4-4-0s which may have been ordered in April 1888 for the **Intercolonial Railway of Canada.** On March 19th 1889 both IRC 146 and 160 were extensively damaged in a head-on collision near Rimouski, Quebec. IRC 146 was retired prior to October 1914, but not sold for scrap until 1917 to the Canadian Car & Foundry in Amherst, Nova Scotia. It was dismantled by the CC&F in 1918. In 1910 IRC 160 was used by the contractor Corbett & Fleisch, building a section of the National Transcontinental Railway between Berrys Mills and Minto, New Brunswick. Before being condemned in 1917, it was rented to the Inverness Railway & Coal Company on Cape Breton Island.

CNR 105-107 — 4-4-0 EIGHT-WHEEL TYPE — A-3-b

Cylinder	Gear	Driv.	Pressure	Boiler	T.E.	Haulage	Appliances Steam	Stkr.	Weights Drivers/Eng./Total	Fuel Capacity Water	Fuel	Length	Notes
18x24"	S	62"	160#	EWT	17120		sat		62/ 97/169000	2700 gals	6 tons	51-11'	[orig]
18x24"	S	63"	150#	EWT	15750	16%	sat		62/ 97/169000	2700 gals	6 tons	51-11'	[107]

Canadian Locomotive & Engine Company (Dübs) 1888 (C-27) $11,700 — (3) Acquired by CNR 9-01-1919

	Serial	Shipped	New as	1-04-1912	by 10-1914	12-1915	7-1917	Retired	Disposition	To
			—	D4 157%		A2-4 80%				
—	340	6-22-88	IRC 34/3	IRC 1032		IRC 1032	Ls IR&C 7	12-18-17	Sc -18 AK	
—	341	6-30-88	IRC 81/2	IRC 1097	Retired				Ss -17 AK	CC&F
105	342	7-09-88	**IRC 174**	**IRC 1034**	Retired	**IRC 1034**			Sc 10- -22 AK	
—	343	7-20-88	IRC 175	IRC 1035	Retired				Ss -17 AK	CC&F
106	344	7-29-88	**IRC 176**	**IRC 1036**	Retired	**IRC 1036**			So -22 AK	**BdO 106**
—	345	8-03-88	IRC 177	IRC 1037	Retired				Ss -17 AK	CC&F
—	346	8-10-88	IRC 178	IRC 1038	Retired	IRC 1038				**CNR 108**
—	347	8-17-88	IRC 179	IRC 1039	Retired				Ss -17 AK	CC&F
107	348	8-24-88	**IRC 180**	**IRC 1040**	Retired	**IRC 1040**			Sc 3- -25 AK	
—	349	8-31-88	IRC 181	IRC 1041	Retired				Sc by -19 AK?	
—	350	9-07-88	IRC 182	IRC 1042	Retired				Ss -17 AK	CC&F
—	351	9-14-88	IRC 183	IRC 1043	Retired				Ss -17 AK	CC&F
—	352	9-20-88	IRC 82/2	IRC 1098	Retired				Ss -17 AK	CC&F
—	353	9-27-88	IRC 83/2	IRC 1033		IRC 1033		12-18-17	Sc -18 AK	

CNR 105-108 were from an order consisting of fourteen 4-4-0s built for the **Intercolonial Railway of Canada.** IRC 1034-1043 and 1097-1098 were all retired prior to October 1914, but four were restored to service during World War I. The remaining locomotives, except for CGR 1041, were not sold for scrap until 1917 to the Canadian Car & Foundry in Amherst, Nova Scotia. They were all dismantled by the CC&F in 1918.

CNR 106 was sold to the **Bras d'Or Coal Company** and remained in service at Broughton, Cape Breton until it was scrapped by the company in 1934. Issue E of the *CNR Mechanical Department Locomotive Diagrams* sheet for **107** had a note "scrapped June 1924", which may have been the date it was removed from service. Issue F was altered to read "scrapped March 1925".

CNR 108 (as CGR 1038) was damaged in a wreck during the winter of 1916 at Hillsboro, New Brunswick while in service on the **Salisbury & Albert Railway.**

CNR 108 — 4-4-0 EIGHT-WHEEL TYPE — A-3-c

Cylinder	Gear	Driv.	Pressure	Boiler	T.E.	Haulage	Appliances Steam	Stkr.	Weights Drivers/Eng./Total	Fuel Capacity Water	Fuel	Length	Notes
18x24"	S	62"	160#	EWT	17000		sat		62/ 97/169000	2700 gals	6 tons	51-11'	[orig]
18x24"	S	62"	160#	EWT	16786	17%	sat		62/ 97/169000	2700 gals	6 tons	51-11'	[CNR]

Canadian Locomotive & Engine Company (Dübs) 1888 (C-27) $11,700 — (1) Acquired by CNR 9-01-1919

	Serial	Shipped	New as	1-04-1912	by 10-1914	12-1915	Disposition
			—	D4[B] 171%		A2-4[B] 80%	
108	346	8-10-88	**IRC 178**	**IRC 1038**	Retired	**CGR 1038**	Sc 5-31-27 AK

CNR 108: See notes under 105-107 above.

CNR 109-111 — 4-4-0 EIGHT-WHEEL TYPE — A-4-a

Cylinder	Gear	Driv.	Pressure	Boiler	T.E.	Haulage	Appliances Steam	Stkr.	Weights Drivers/Eng./Total	Fuel Capacity Water	Fuel	Length	Notes
17x24"	S	63"	160#	EWT	15000		sat		59/ 88/168000	2700 gals	4½ tons	51-12'	
17x24"	S	63"	160#	EWT	15000		sat		59/ 88/161000	2000 gals	4½ tons	51-6'	[CGR 1917]
17x24"	S	63"	160#	EWT	14840	15%	sat		59/ 88/168000	2000 gals	4½ tons	51-6'	[CNR]

Danforth Locomotive & Machine Company 1880 $9000 — (3) Acquired by CNR 9-01-1919

	Serial	Shipped	New as	rebuilt	1-04-1912	12-1915	Disposition
			—		D19 151%	A2-19 75%	
109	1182	-80	**IRC 109**	2-1896	**IRC 1044**	**CGR 1044**	Sc 2- -23 AK
110	1183	-80	**IRC 110**	7-1896	**IRC 1045**	**CGR 1045**	Sc 5- -23 AK
111	1184	-80	**IRC 111**	3-1896	**IRC 1046**	**CGR 1046**	Sc 11-06-28 AK

CNR 109-111, delivered to the **Intercolonial Railway of Canada,** may have been built as DL&M stock. In 1896 all were rebuilt with new boilers by IRC at Moncton. IRC 1044 was known to have been used on the **Salisbury & Albert Railway.**

CNR 112-115 — 4-4-0 EIGHT-WHEEL TYPE — A-5-a

Cylinder	Gear	Driv.	Pressure	Boiler	T.E.	Haulage	Steam	Stkr.	Drivers/Eng./Total	Water	Coal	Length	Notes
Specifications							Appliances		Weights	Fuel Capacity			
17x24"	S	64"	160#	EWT	15000		sat		59/ 88/168000	2700 gals	5 tons	50-7'	
17x24"	S	64"	160#	EWT	15000		sat		59/ 88/166500	2500 gals	5 tons	50-7'	[CGR 1917]
17x24"	S	62"	160#	EWT	14739	15%	sat		59/ 88/168000	2000 gals	5 tons	51-1'	[112]
17x24"	S	63"	160#	EWT	14300	15%	sat		59/ 88/161000	2000 gals	5 tons	51-1'	[115]

Hinkley Locomotive Company 1880 $9000 — (4) Acquired by CNR 9-01-1919

	Serial	Shipped	New as	Rebuilt	1-04-1912	1914	12-1915	6-1918	Disposition	To
			—		D8 151%	So	A2-8 75%	A2-8 75%		
112	—	6- -80	**IRC 112**	6-1897	**IRC 1047**		**CGR 1047**		Sc 9-30-28 AK	
(113)	—	7- -80	**IRC 113**	7-1897	**IRC 1048**		**CGR 1048**		So 2-18-22 AK	**KNR 6**
114	—	7- -80	**IRC 114**	6-1897	**IRC 1049**	**M&B 3**		**CGR 1049**	Sc 6- -22 AK	
115	—	7- -80	**IRC 115**	9-1897	**IRC 1050**		**CGR 1050**		Sc 10- -22 AK	

A-5-a

M&B first 3 (in this photo), was an unrebuilt Manchester, formerly IRC 138, bought by M&B about 1910 and was never repaired after the wreck at Scotch Settlement in February 1914. The date of the photo on page A-5 would be shortly after acquisition around 1910. [MONCTON MUSEUM/CONRAD STEEVES COLLECTION]

CNR 112-115, built for the **Intercolonial Railway of Canada**, were rebuilt with new boilers by IRC at Moncton. CGR 1048, assigned to **113**, was never renumbered or relettered before its sale to the **Kent Northern Railway.** It was scrapped in 1929, not being brought back into stock when the CNR purchased the KNR on June 14th 1929. **CNR 112** was planned for removal in 1925, but was returned to service the same year.

CNR 114 (as CGR 1049) was apparently sold in either 1914 or 1915 to the **Moncton and Buctouche Railway.** It was condemned December 18th 1917, but when the M&B was acquired by the Government of Canada and turned over to the CGR for operation on June 1st 1918, it was returned to service on September 4th 1918 as CGR 1049. It was finally removed from service in 1920 and scrapped as 114 in 1922.

The last surviving member of this lot built by Hinkley was in the scrap line at Moncton in 1928. The only changes to 112's appearance and those of M&B 3 were created by technological improvements, notably the advances in lighting, the relocation of the sand dome and installation of an air pump on the running board. A metal plate below the windows of the wooden cab solved the problem of standardized lettering on the older style of panelling. [*CNR LOCOMOTIVE DATA CARD*]

CNR 116 — 4-4-0 EIGHT-WHEEL TYPE — A-6-a

Specifications							Appliances		Weights	Fuel Capacity		Length	Notes
Cylinder	Gear	Driv.	Pressure	Boiler	T.E.	Haulage	Steam	Stkr.	Drivers/Eng./Total	Water	Fuel		
18x24"	S	62"	150#		15990	16%	sat		64/101/169540	2980 gals	tons	- '	[CaNoR 1909]

Baldwin Locomotive Works – Burnham, Parry, Williams & Company 1887 — (1) Acquired by CNR 9-01-1919

	Serial	Shipped	New as	1898	7-1901	1907	1-1912	Disposition
			—	B	—	—	A-6-A 15%	
116	8689	9-16-87	**NP 423**	**NP 670**	**CaNoR 17**/1	**CaNoR 51**	**CaNoR 23**	Sc 9- -22 PK

CNR 116 was one of twenty-two 4-4-0s built for the **Northern Pacific Railway** as **403-424**. Baldwin records give the build-date as July 1887, but the date used in the roster is from CaNoR records – likely the date received by NP.

CNR 117 — 4-4-0 EIGHT-WHEEL TYPE — A-7-a

Specifications							Appliances		Weights	Fuel Capacity		Length	Notes
Cylinder	Gear	Driv.	Pressure	Boiler	T.E.	Haulage	Steam	Stkr.	Drivers/Eng./Total	Water	Fuel		
17x24"	S	64"	145#		13000	13%	sat		52/ 80/ 000	gals	tons	- '	

Rogers Locomotive Works 1889 — (1) Acquired by CNR 9-01-1919

	Serial	Shipped	New as	1902	1-1912	Disposition
			—	—	A-7-A 13%	
(117)	4128	4- -89	**CRNS 3 MIDDLETON**	**H&SW 3**	**CaNoR 24**	Sc 3-31-22 AK

CNR 117 was built as a single locomotive order for the **Central Railway of Nova Scotia.** The company was reorganized as the **Halifax and South Western Railway** and later operated by the **Canadian Northern Railway.**

CNR 118 — 4-4-0 EIGHT-WHEEL TYPE — A-8-a

Cylinder	Gear	Driv.	Pressure	Boiler	T.E.	Haulage	Steam	Stkr.	Drivers/Eng./Total	Water	Coal	Length	Notes
Specifications							Appliances		Weights	Fuel Capacity			
17x24"	S	60"	130#		15000		sat		/ 91/ 000	gals	tons	- '	[orig]
17x24"	S	62"	160#	WT	14300	15%	sat		56/ 84/146350	2600 gals	4½ tons	52-0'	[118]

Fleming & Humbert Foundry 1883 (unofficial serial numbers) $13,900 — (1) Acquired by CNR 9-01-1919

	Serial	Shipped	New as	Rebuilt	1-04-1912	12-1915	Retired	Disposition	To
			—		D11^D 152%	A2-11^D 60%			
—	(27)	1- -83	IRC 135	9-1897 AK	IRC 1072 (D11^A)		af 10-1914	Sc by -17 AK	
118	(28)	2- -83	**IRC 136**	2-1901 AK	**IRC 1073**	**CGR 1073**	af 6-1924	Sc 5- -25 AK	
—	(29)	2- -83	IRC 137	12-1895 AK	IRC 1074 (D11^B)		af 10-1914	Ss - -17 AK	CC&F

CNR 118 was the second of three built as **Intercolonial Railway of Canada** 135-137. All acquired new boilers during their rebuilds, but only the boiler for IRC 136 had a pressure of 160 PSI. The *CNR Mechanical Department Locomotive Diagrams* sheet shows it scrapped in June 1924, but this was the date it was removed from service. At the time of its retirement it was the sole surviving Fleming-built locomotive.

The boiler of IRC 137 was exchanged with IRC 4-4-0 154 in 1895 at Moncton. Both IRC 1072 and 1074 were retired sometime after 1914, but only 1074 was sold for scrap to the Canadian Car & Foundry in Amherst, Nova Scotia. It was believed to have been dismantled by the CC&F in 1918.

CNR 119 — 4-4-0 EIGHT-WHEEL TYPE — first A-9-a

Cylinder	Gear	Driv.	Pressure	Boiler	T.E.	Haulage	Steam	Stkr.	Drivers/Eng./Total	Water	Coal	Length	Notes
Specifications							Appliances		Weights	Fuel Capacity			
17x24"	S	61"	140#	WT	14000	14%	sat		54/ 93/168000	3000 gals	tons	- '	[CaNoR 1913]
16x24"	S	59"	140#	WT	11760	13%	sat		57/ 86/153000	3000 gals	8 tons	52-4'	[CNR]

Brooks Locomotive Company 1887 (253) — (1) Acquired by CNR 9-01-1919

	Serial	Shipped	New as	1900	7-1906	8-1906	1-1912	Disposition	To	1923
			—	C-22	—	—	A-9-A 13%		—	V
(119)	1199	5- -87	**SP&D 49**	**NP 1118**	**CaNoR 40**	**CNQ 40**	**CaNoR 27**	So -22 AK	**D&V 27; QRL&P 11**	

CNR 119 was one of fourteen built for the **St. Paul & Duluth Railroad** as 40-53 (#1194-1203), a forerunner of the **Northern Pacific Railway**. After a month in **Canadian Northern Railway** service, it was relettered for the **Canadian Northern Quebec Railway**. It was reported sold as **CaNoR 27** to **Disentis & Villeneuve** (CNR spelling) for either resale to, or directly to the **Quebec Railway Light & Power** in 1923. It was retired for scrap by the QRL&P in October 1927.

St. Paul & Duluth Railroad 45 was the one chosen in the order of fourteen for the builder's portrait at Dunkirk in May 1887. By the time SP&D 49 became Quebec Railway Light & Power's number 11 thirty-six years later, its appearance would have been significantly altered. The diamond stack would have been replaced when fuel was changed from wood to coal. The kerosene-fuelled headlight casing would have been reduced in size, especially if conversion to electricity had taken place. Another victim of change was the wood stave pilot. It would have been rebuilt with footboards or boiler tubes. The changes in the specification record imply the cylinders and drivers were also replaced. [BROOKS WORKS PHOTO B-19/ALCO HISTORIC PHOTOS]

CNR 120-122 — 4-4-0 EIGHT-WHEEL TYPE — A-20-a

Specifications							Appliances		Weights	Fuel Capacity		Length	Notes
Cylinder	Gear	Driv.	Pressure	Boiler	T.E.	Haulage	Steam	Stkr.	Drivers/Eng./Total	Water	Fuel		
18x24"	S	63"	180#	WT	18880	19%	sat		75/115/190000	3800 gals	6 tons	51-1'	[CaNoR 1913]
18x24"	S	63"	180#	EWT	18885	18%	sat		75/103/198000	4000 gals	8 tons	51-1'	[CNR]

Canadian Locomotive Company 1904; 1906 $9500 — (3) Acquired by CNR 9-01-1919

	Serial	Shipped	New as	4-1909	1-1912	Disposition
			—	—	A-20-A 18%	
120	615	6-02-04	**COR 14**	**MM&Co (CaNoR) COR 47**	**CaNoR 47**	Sc 3-31-25 MV
121	628	5-23-04	**COR 15***	**MM&Co (CaNoR) COR 48**	**CaNoR 48**	Sc 7-15-25 EH
122	746	10-15-06	**COR 16**	**MM&Co (CaNoR) COR 49**	**CaNoR 49**	Sc 3-30-25 MV

CNR 120-122 were from three orders for single locomotives delivered to the **Central Ontario Railway.** They were acquired in the purchase of the COR by the **Mackenzie, Mann & Company Limited**, renumbered into the **Canadian Northern Railway** system in 1912, and finally transferred to the CaNoR for operation in July 1914.

COR 15 (121), at Kingston in May 1904, and its mate shipped in June, was built relatively late in the development of the 4-4-0, but both would well suit the needs of the railway which ordered them.
[CLC LITHOGRAPH/DON McQUEEN COLLECTION]

CaNoR 49 (122) was built for the COR a bit more than two years later and was the third last 4-4-0 to be built by the CLC. (The last pair were to follow in 1908 for the Quebec Central). The soft focussed photograph was taken at an unidentified location in eastern Ontario before 1919. By that time it had been upgraded with a turbo-generator for the electrical systems, had the cab's forward side windows blanked, and extensions built onto the tender's coal bunker.
[H.L. GOLDSMITH/GEORGE CARPENTER COLLECTION]

A-20-a

CNR 123-124 — 4-4-0 EIGHT-WHEEL TYPE — A-24-a

Cylinder	Gear	Driv.	Pressure	Boiler	T.E.	Haulage	Steam	Stkr.	Drivers/Eng./Total	Water	Coal	Length	Notes
Specifications							Appliances		Weights	Fuel Capacity			
17x24"	S	62"	160#		15000		sat		55/ 87/149000	3600 gals	6 tons	52-0½'	[orig]
17x24"	S	62"	150#	WT	14300	14%	sat		55/ 87/147000	3600 gals	8 tons	52-0½'	[CaNoR 1913]
17x24"	S	62"	150#	WT	14037	14%	sat		55/ 87/161500	4000 gals	8 tons	52-0½'	[CNR]

Locomotive & Machine Company of Montreal 1904 (Q-7) & 1906 (Q-44) $7500 (Q-44) (2) Acquired by CNR 9-01-1919

	Serial	Shipped	New as	1910	1-1912	Disposition
			—	—	A-24-A 15%	
(123)	29907	6- -04	**BW&NW 66***	**(CaNoR) BW&NW 66**	**(CaNoR) BW&NW 53**	Sc 3-13-22 MV
124	40667	8- -06	**BW&NW 67**	**(CaNoR) BW&NW 67**	**(CaNoR) BW&NW 54**	Sc 8-27-31 AK

CNR 123 and 124 were from two orders for the **Brockville Westport & North Western Railway**. The road eventually came under the control of the **Canadian Northern Railway**. CNR 124 was equipped with fire-fighting apparatus in June 1925 after it was transferred to the Atlantic region.

BW&NW 66 (123), at Montreal in June 1904, was the first of two new 4-4-0s built for the ambitious eastern Ontario railway which had at first planned to build as far west as Sault Ste. Marie. The wagon top boiler with an extended smokebox and an air pump on the engineer's side were distinctive features of the fourth last saturated 4-4-0 built at Montreal. (Two for the Quebec Central were delivered the same year). [MLW PHOTO Q-7/GEORGE CARPENTER COLLECTION]

BW&NW 54 (124), at Brockville's Church Street station after 1912, may have had the CaNoR class stencilled on the cab, but the remainder of the markings proclaimed the short line's semi-independence. The set of deer antlers ahead of the headlamp chimney vent provided a personal touch to the last saturated 4-4-0 built by MLW. [CHARLES SHERIDAN/DON McQUEEN COLLECTION]

CNR 125 — 4-4-0 EIGHT-WHEEL TYPE — A-25-a

Specifications							Appliances		Weights	Fuel Capacity		Length	Notes
Cylinder	Gear	Driv.	Pressure	Boiler	T.E.	Haulage	Steam	Stkr.	Drivers/Eng./Total	Water	Fuel		
17x24"	S	62"	145#	WT	13775	14%	sat		58/ 90/ 000	gals	tons	- '	[CaNoR 1913]
16x24"	S	63"	140#	WT	11660	13%	sat		69/102/196700	4000 gals	8 tons	55-6'	[CNR]

Rathbun Company	1890?	(unofficial serial numbers)	Rebuilt by Rathbun 1893?			(1) Acquired by CNR 9-01-1919
	Serial	Shipped	New as	Rebuilt?	1-1912	Disposition
			—		A-25-A 15%	
125	(1)	-90?	**BQR 1**	1893?	**(CaNoR) BQR 55**	Sc 2- -23 EH

CNR 125 had no builder or build-date documentation, although the *CNR Mechanical Department Locomotive Diagrams* sheet listed the builder as CLC, and some copies had a manuscripted date of 1897 added. Some CaNoR stock books have "Rebuilt by Rathbun", but the original builder was not identified, while others had the entry "Deseron' 1897". From what records are available, it may have been assembled at Deseronto for the **Bay of Quinte Railway** using new parts from the Canadian Locomotive & Engine Company and older material from Rathbun sources. If so, this may have given rise to the later notion it was a rebuild.

Judging from the shine of the varnish on the sides of the tender and cab, **BQR 1** (125) at Deseronto, Ontario was photographed when built in either in 1890 or 1893. The possibility parts may have been supplied by CLC is strengthened by the fact this 4-4-0 and BQR 5, built by the Kingston firm in February 1893, had near-identical physical appearances. The design and placement of steam and sand domes, the wagon top boiler, design of cab, and the inclusion of driving wheel splash guards, are common to both. BQR 5 differed in that it had a capped stack. The builder's photograph of BQR 5 can be found in McQueen and Thomson: *Constructed In Kingston*, page 195. [FAIRBURN PHOTO/W.D. (BILL) THOMSON COLLECTION]

CNR 126-127 (first) — 4-4-0 EIGHT-WHEEL TYPE — A-26-a

Specifications							Appliances		Weights	Fuel Capacity		Length	Notes
Cylinder	Gear	Driv.	Pressure	Boiler	T.E.	Haulage	Steam	Stkr.	Drivers/Eng./Total	Water	Fuel		
17x24"	S	62"	145#	WT	13775	14%	sat		56/ 88/168300	2500 gals	6 tons	55-7'	[CaNoR 1913]
17x24"	S	62"	140#	WT	13310	13%	sat		55/ 88/168300	2500 gals	6 tons	55-7'	[CNR]

Rathbun Company	1890?; 1892	(unofficial serial numbers)	Rebuilt by Rathbun 1893?				(2) Acquired by CNR 9-01-1919
	Serial	Shipped	New as	Rebuilt?	1-1912	4-1914	Disposition
			—		A-26-A 13%	A-26-A 13%	
126/1	(2)	9- -90?	**BQR 2**	1893?	**(CaNoR) BQR 56**		Sc -22 AK
127/1	(3)	8-25-92	**BQR 6/2?**	1893?	**(CaNoR) BQR 57**	Leased **S&AR**	Sc 10-29-20 MV

CNR 126 (first) had no builder or build-date documentation, although CaNoR *Locomotive Data* (1913) and *CNR Mechanical Department Locomotive Diagrams* sheets had the builder as "R.Co Deseron" in 1893. Other CaNoR stock books have "Rebuilt by Rathbun", but the original builder was not recorded. From what records are available, it may have been assembled at Deseronto for the **Bay of Quinte Railway** using new parts from the Canadian Locomotive & Engine Company and older material from Rathbun sources, giving the impression later it was a rebuild.

(text continues on next page)

CNR 127 (first) has been documented as built by Rathbun at Deseronto using Canadian Locomotive & Engine Company parts and put into service for the **Bay of Quinte Railway**. According to records of the Toronto & York Radial Railway, it was in operation (still lettered BQR) in April 1914 on the **Schomberg & Aurora Railway**, a steam operated line controlled by the electrified Toronto & York Radial Railway.

Even though the location and date of the photograph of **BQR 56** (126) is unclear, the train may have been at either Deseronto or Napanee. The installation of the pilot snowplow and bare tree branches suggest a late fall portrait of the railway readying for an Eastern Ontario winter. The CaNoR smokebox number plate, road number and class lettering help bracket the date between 1912 and 1919. Although the 4-4-0 was transferred by either CaNoR or CNR to the Maritimes, it only remained on the CNR roster for three years.
[AL PATERSON COLLECTION]

CNR 126 (second) — 4-4-0 EIGHT-WHEEL TYPE — second A-9-a

Cylinder	Gear	Driv.	Pressure	Boiler	T.E.	Haulage	Steam	Stkr.	Drivers/Eng./Total	Water	Coal	Length	Notes
Specifications							Appliances		Weights	Fuel Capacity			
17x22"	S	63"	140#	ST	12000		sat		75/134/134232	gals	tons	40-8'	[4-4-2T]
17x22"	S	63"	140#	ST	12009	12%	sat		53/ 87/ 000	2500 gals	10 tons	54-9'	[4-4-0]

Grand Trunk Railway – Pointe St. Charles 1883 as 4-4-2T; Rebuilt by GTR in 1888 to 4-4-0 $10,000 (1) Acquired by CNR 3-01-1923

	Serial	Shipped	New as	1888	1898	11-1904	11-1904	1-1910	1-1910	Mods	Disposition	To
			4-4-2T	4-4-0	—	K1	L	K1	L			
—	1120	5- -83	GTR 190		GTR 266	GTR 201		GTR 1526			Sc 9- -14	
—	1121	5- -83	GTR 191		GTR 267	GTR 202		GTR 1527				**CNR 41**
—	1122	6- -83	GTR 192		GTR 268	GTR 203		GTR 1528			Sc 5- -17	
—	1123	6- -83	GTR 193	GTR 193	GTR 261						So 2- -02	**MRNS**
—	1124	6- -83	GTR 194	GTR 194	GTR 262		GTR 197		GTR 1994		Sc 8- -18	
—	1125	6- -83	GTR 195	GTR 195	GTR 263		GTR 198		GTR 1995		Sc 4- -11	
126/2	1126	7- -83	**GTR 196**	GTR 196	**GTR 264**		**GTR 199**		**GTR 1996**	p	Sc 8- -25 HQ	
—	1127	7- -83	GTR 197		GTR 269	GTR 204		GTR 1529			Sc 11- -17	
—	1128	7- -83	GTR 198	GTR 198	GTR 265		GTR 200		GTR 1997		So 12- -19	**PR&Q**
—	1129	8- -83	GTR 199		GTR 270	GTR 205		GTR 1530			Sc 9- -19	

CNR 126 (second) was one of ten 4-4-2T Types built by the **Grand Trunk Railway of Canada**, two of which became **CNR 41** and **126**. Five were rebuilt in 1888 as 4-4-0s, and all but two were removed from the GTR roster between 1902 and 1919. **CNR 126** (as GTR 1996) was equipped with a rear pilot (p) in December 1921.

GTR 261 was sold to the Midland Railway of Nova Scotia and GTR 1997 to John Breakey's Phillipsburg Railway & Quarry Company in Quebec.

CNR 127 (second) 4-4-0 EIGHT-WHEEL TYPE A-10-a

Specifications							Appliances		Weights	Fuel Capacity		Length	Notes
Cylinder	Gear	Driv.	Pressure	Boiler	T.E.	Haulage	Steam	Stkr.	Drivers/Eng./Total	Water	Fuel		
17x24"	S	60"	145#		13000		sat		52/ / 000	gals	tons	- '	[orig]
17x24"	S	64"	135#	WT	12000		sat		52/ 81/ 000	gals	tons	- '	[rblt] *(a)*
17x24"	S	64"	135#	ST	12000		sat		52/ 81/ 000	gals	tons	53-0'	[rblt] *(b)*
17x24"	S	64"	145#	WT	14000		sat		52/ 81/ 000	gals	tons	53-0'	[rblt] *(c)*
17x24"	S	63"	145#	WT	12000		sat		52/ 81/ 000	gals	tons	53-0'	[rblt] *(d)*
17x24"	S	63"	140#	WT	14000	14%	sat		52/ 81/ 000	gals	tons	53-0'	[127]

Manchester Locomotive Company 1873 $13,750 — (1) Acquired by CNR 3-01-1923

	Serial	Shipped	New as	()-1882	1-1884	6-1889	nB	1898	11-1904	1-1910	Disposition	To
			—	—	—	—		—	J2	J2		
—	591	8- -73	GTR 150								Wr 5- -87	
—	592	8- -73	GTR 151			GTR 179	1898 *c*	GTR 466	GTR 264	GTR 2036	Sc 6- -19	
—	593	8- -73	GTR 152			GTR 182	1898 *c*	GTR 469	GTR 267	GTR 2039	Sc 10-12-16	
—	594	8- -73	GTR 153	MRC 20(4)	GTR 620		— *a*	GTR 485	GTR 283	GTR 2053	Sc 5- -18	
—	595	8- -73	GTR 154								Wr 2- -86	
—	596	9- -73	GTR 155					GTR 293			So 10- -02	**IB&O 3**
—	597	9- -73	GTR 156				1897 *c*	GTR 281	■ GTR 245	GTR 2021	Sc 12- -18 HQ	
—	598	9- -73	GTR 157		Ls: MRC 157		1891 *b*	GTR 334	GTR 246	GTR 2022	Sc 7-17-16	
—	599	9- -73	GTR 158					GTR 451			Sc 9- -04	
—	600	9- -73	GTR 159					GTR 452			Sc 6- -99	
—	601	9- -73	GTR 160	MRC 25(8)	GTR 625			GTR 490	GTR 287		Sc 6- -07	
—	602	9- -73	GTR 161					GTR 454			Sc 8- -02	
—	603	9- -73	GTR 162	MRC 26(8)	GTR 626		1897 *c*	GTR 491	GTR 288	GTR 2057	Sc 5- -18	
—	604	9- -73	GTR 163				1895 *c*	GTR 294	GTR 238	GTR 2014	Sc 12- -18 HQ	
—	605	9- -73	GTR 164	MRC 34(8)	GTR 634			GTR 492			Sc 10- -03	
—	606	9- -73	GTR 165	MRC 24(7)	GTR 624		1897 *c*	GTR 489	GTR 286	GTR 2056	Sc 10-12-16	
—	607	9- -73	GTR 166				— *a*	GTR 458	GTR 257	GTR 2030	Sc 7-17-16	
—	608	10- -73	GTR 167				1894 *d*	GTR 297	GTR 241	GTR 2017	Sc 6-30-19 HQ	
—	609	10- -73	GTR 168	MRC 23(6)	GTR 623			GTR 488			Sc 4- -03	
—	610	10- -73	GTR 169				1889 *b*	GTR 335	GTR 247	GTR 2023	Sc 5- -18	
127/2	611	10- -73	**GTR 170**				1881; 1895 *c*	**GTR 295**	**GTR 239**	**GTR 2015**	Sc 9- -23 MP	
—	612	10- -73	GTR 171					GTR 460			Sc 8- -02	
—	613	10- -73	GTR 172	MRC 19(4)	GTR 619		— *a*	GTR 484	GTR 282	GTR 2052	Sc 6-03-15	
—	614	10- -73	GTR 173					GTR 462	GTR 260		Sc 6- -07	
—	615	10- -73	GTR 174				1895 *d*	GTR 296	GTR 240	GTR 2016	Sc 6-03-15	
—	616	10- -73	GTR 175				— *a*	GTR 463	GTR 261	GTR 2033	Sc 10-12-16	

■ GTR 325 1-1901 to 11-1904

A-10-a

Although neither of the illustrated pair became CNR stock, they represented two lots built by Manchester in 1873. MRC 157 at Lindsay in 1884 and CNR 127 were built as freight 4-4-0s with 64-inch drivers. Although lettered Midland, the 157 was leased from the GTR but retained its owner's road number. [SIRMAN COLLECTION]

GTR 413, at Alexandria, Ontario in 1893, and CNR 128 were built as passenger locomotives with 69-inch drivers. [H.L. GOLDSMITH/GEORGE CARPENTER COLLECTION]

CNR 127 (second) was one of twenty-six 4-4-0s built for the **Grand Trunk Railway of Canada. CNR 127** had two boiler replacements during its lifetime as GTR 170, its first in June 1881, and the second in 1895.

The seven sold to the Midland Railway of Canada returned to the GTR after the amalgamation with the MRC. There is evidence at least one more was leased to the road. GTR 293 was sold to the Irondale Bancroft & Ottawa Railway.

CNR 128 — 4-4-0 EIGHT-WHEEL TYPE — A-10-a

Specifications							Appliances		Weights	Fuel Capacity		Length	Notes
Cylinder	Gear	Driv.	Pressure	Boiler	T.E.	Haulage	Steam	Stkr.	Drivers/Eng./Total	Water	Coal		
17x24"	S	60"	145#		00		sat		/ / 000	gals	tons	- '	[orig.]
17x24"	S	69"	145#	WT	12000		sat		52/ 81/ 000	gals	tons	53-0'	[rblt] *(e)*
17x24"	S	69"	145#	WT	12000		sat		52/ 81/ 000	gals	tons	56-2'	[rblt] *(f)*
17x24"	S	69"	135#	ST	11000		sat		32/ 81/ 000	gals	tons	53-0'	[rblt] *(g)*
17x24"	S	63"	145#	WT	12000	12%	sat		52/ 81/ 000	gals	tons	56-2'	[rblt] *(h)*

Manchester Locomotive Company 1873 $13,750 — (1) Acquired by CNR 3-01-1923

(1)	Serial	Shipped	New as	nB	1898	11-1904	1-1910	c.1920 to c.8-1923	Disposition
			—		—	J2	J2	J2	
—	633	11- -73	GTR 406		GTR 476	(GTR 274)			Sc 12- -04
—	634	11- -73	GTR 407	1895 *f*	GTR 310	GTR 244	GTR 2020		Sc 5- -20
—	635	11- -73	GTR 408	1897 *g*	GTR 349	GTR 249	GTR 2025		Sc 6- -19
—	636	11- -73	GTR 409	1897 *e*	GTR 477	GTR 275	GTR 2045		So 6- -16
—	637	11- -73	GTR 410		GTR 478	GTR 276	GTR 2046		Sc 4- -11
—	638	11- -73	GTR 411		GTR 299				Wr 1- -01
—	639	11- -73	GTR 412	1897 *h*	GTR 479	GTR 277	GTR 2047		Sc 5- -18
—	640	11- -73	GTR 413	1894 *f*	GTR 480	GTR 278	GTR 2048		Sc 6-03-15
128	641	11- -73	**GTR 414**	1900 *h*	**GTR 481**	**GTR 279**	**GTR 2049**	- Leased to **TIR** -	Sc 6- -25 HQ
—	642	11- -73	GTR 415	1894 *h*	GTR 300	GTR 243	GTR 2019		Sc 8- -18

CNR 128 was one of ten 4-4-0s built for the **Grand Trunk Railway of Canada. CNR 128** was rebuilt twice, once in April 1883 as GTR 414, and again as GTR 279 in 1909. It was leased to the **Thousand Islands Railway** to replace GTR 2005 and 2020 and remained on lease until the arrival of CNR 42 in 1923.

CNR 129 — 4-4-0 EIGHT-WHEEL TYPE — A-11-a

Specifications							Appliances		Weights	Fuel Capacity		Length	Notes
Cylinder	Gear	Driv.	Pressure	Boiler	T.E.	Haulage	Steam	Stkr.	Drivers/Eng./Total	Water	Fuel		
16x24"	S	54"	#		00		sat		/ / 300	gals	tons	- '	[orig]
16x24"	S	58"	#		00		sat		/ / 000	gals	tons	- '	[GTR final specs] *(e)*
16x24"	S	63"	#		00		sat		/ / 000	gals	tons	- '	[GTR final specs] *(c)*
17x24"	S	69"	140#	ST	13000		sat		47/ 74/ 000	gals	tons	53-6'	[GTR final specs] *(f)*
17x24"	S	63"	140#	ST	13000		sat		48/ 76/ 000	gals	tons	53-6'	[GTR final specs] *(g)*

Rhode Island Locomotive Company 1870; Rebuilt by Canadian Locomotive & Engine Company 1-1883 $13,000 (1) Acquired by CNR 3-01-1923

	Serial	Shipped	New as	8-1882	1898	12-1902	11-1904	11-1904	1-1910		Disposition	To
			—	—	—	—	J4	N	J4			
—	241	12- -70	GWR 132	GTR 772	GTR 69	GTR 156		GTR 123		*c*	Sc 7- -09	
(129)	242	12-12-70	**GWR 134**	**GTR 773**	**GTR 171**	**GTR 371**	**GTR 360**		**GTR 2067**	*g*	Sc 12- -24 LM	
—	243	12- -70	GWR 136	GTR 774	GTR 51	GTR 139		GTR 139		*c*	Sc 6- -06	
—	244	12- -70	GWR 138/1 ■	GTR 756	GTR 370		GTR 312(J3)		GTR 2128(J3)	*f*	Sc 10- -22	
—	245	12- -70	GWR 140	GTR 776	GTR 173	GTR 173		GTR 145		*c*	Sc 10- -09	
—	246	12-17-70	GWR 142	GTR 777	GTR 34	GTR 119	GTR 292(J3)		GTR 2123(J3)	*f*		**CNR 135**
—	247	12- -70	GWR 144	GTR 778	GTR 31	GTR 113		GTR 113		*e*	Sc 6- -06	
—	248	12- -70	GWR 146	GTR 779	GTR 174	GTR 174		GTR 146		*c*	Sc 6- -06	
—	249	12- -70	GWR 148/1								Rs by- -72	

■ To GWR 211 by 1-1873

CNR 129 was one of nine standard gauge freight 4-4-0s built as **Great Western Railway of Canada 132-148** which after amalgamation became **Grand Trunk Railway of Canada** locomotives. **GTR 773** was one of three rebuilt (including new boilers) in January 1883 at the CL&ECo., although the GTR record showed the Kingston company building them as new locomotives.

CNR 130-131 — 4-4-0 EIGHT-WHEEL TYPE — A-12-a

Specifications							Appliances		Weights	Fuel Capacity		Length	Notes
Cylinder	Gear	Driv.	Pressure	Boiler	T.E.	Haulage	Steam	Stkr.	Drivers/Eng./Total	Water	Fuel		
18x24"	S	63"	150#	ST	16000		sat		/ / 000	gals	tons	- '	[orig]
17x24"	S	63"	150#	ST	14037	14%	sat		56/ 93/160910	3000 gals	10 tons	55-0'	[CNR]

Canadian Locomotive & Engine Company 1886-1887 (C-19) $13,000 (2) Acquired by CNR 3-01-1923

	Serial	Shipped	New as	1888	1898	1899	11-1904	11-1904	1-1910	1-1910	Disposition	To
			—	—	—	—	H1	H9	H1	H9		
—	310	11- -86	N&NW 81	GTR 684	GTR 525			GTR 406		GTR 2070	Sc 6- -16	
—	311	-86	N&NW 82	GTR 685	GTR 526			GTR 398		GTR 2068	Sc 6- -19	
—	312	-86	N&NW 83	GTR 686	GTR 527	GTR 571	GTR 443		GTR 1909			**CNR 314**
—	313	12-28-86	N&NW 84	GTR 687	GTR 528	GTR 572	GTR 444		GTR 1910			**CNR 315**
130	314	12-31-86	**N&NW 85**	**GTR 688**	**GTR 529**			**GTR 399**		**GTR 2069**	Sc 2-10-25 LM	
131	315	12-31-87	**N&NW 86**	**GTR 689**	**GTR 530**			**GTR 407**		**GTR 2073**	Sc 3-24-25 HQ	
—	316	1-10-87	N&NW 87*	GTR 690	GTR 531			GTR 400		GTR 2071	Sc 9- -19	
—	317	2-01-87	N&NW 88	GTR 691	GTR 532			GTR 401		GTR 2072	Sc 8- -19	

N&NW 87 at Kingston before delivery in January 1887, was without headlight or pilot and sub-lettered N&PJ underneath the owner's identification on the cab. [CL&ECO. PHOTO/ QUEEN'S UNIVERSITY ARCHIVES/DON McQUEEN COLLECTION]

GTR 401 outside Pointe St. Charles shops in Montreal during July 1905 had undergone dome replacements and acquired different driving wheel counterbalances. Only two from this 1887 order became CNR stock.
[C.A. BUTCHER/WES DENGATE COLLECTION]

CNR 130 and **131** were two of six 4-4-0s built for the **Northern & North Western Railway of Canada** before the road's amalgamation with the **Grand Trunk Railway of Canada.** Two others which had been rebuilt with altered specifications became **314** and **315**.

Northern & Pacific Junction Railway 87 and **88** were in an add-on order to C-19 for N&NW 81-86. GTR 2072 was sold to R.T. Gilman in 1919. About 1926 it became Morrow & Beatty number 1, and may also have been at Fitzroy, Ontario with Morrow & Beatty, building an HEPC facility. Even though the Spruce Falls Power & Paper Company roster seemed not to have assigned the number 101 to a locomotive, the 4-4-0 is believed to have been SFP&P 101.

GTR 2196 at Pointe St. Charles about 1910, was one of a pair which came from a 1888 order for the N&NW. It finished its career equipped with GTR's distinctive torpedo-shaped domes and different styles of driver counterweights. Its mate was assigned road number 132 by the CNR in 1923.
[GTR PHOTO/GEORGE CARPENTER COLLECTION]

CNR 132 — 4-4-0 EIGHT-WHEEL TYPE — A-12-a

Cylinder	Gear	Driv.	Pressure	Boiler	T.E.	Haulage	Steam	Stkr.	Weights Drivers/Eng./Total	Water	Fuel	Length	Notes
18x24"	S	63"	150#	ST	16000		sat		/ / 000	gals	tons	- '	[orig]
17x24"	S	63"	150#	ST	14037	14%	sat		56/ 93/160910	3000 gals	10 tons	55-0'	[CNR]

Canadian Locomotive & Engine Company 1888 (C-19) $13,000 — (1) Acquired by CNR 3-01-1923

	Serial	Shipped	New as	1888	1898	11-1904	1-1910	To	Disposition
			—	—	—	H9	H9	17x24"	
(132)	333	-88	**N&NW 73**	**GTR 682**	**GTR 523**	**GTR 404**	**GTR 2195**	9-18 HQ	Sc 8- -25 HQ
—	334	-88	N&NW 74	GTR 683	GTR 524	GTR 405	GTR 2196		Sc 5- -18

CNR 132 was one of two built for the **Northern & North Western Railway of Canada** before the company was amalgamated with the **Grand Trunk Railway of Canada.** It was rebuilt to 17x24" specifications by Pointe St. Charles in September 1918.

CNR 133 — 4-4-0 EIGHT-WHEEL TYPE — A-13-a

Cylinder	Gear	Driv.	Pressure	Boiler	T.E.	Haulage	Steam	Stkr.	Weights Drivers/Eng./Total	Water	Fuel	Length	Notes
17x24"	S	63"	140#	ST	13000	13%	sat		49/ 76/ 000	gals	tons	52-11'	

The Portland Company 1880 $12,000 — (1) Acquired by CNR 3-01-1923

	Serial	Shipped	New as	1882	1-1884	1898	To	1-1910	Disposition
			—	—	—	—	J5	J5	
133	368	9-18-80	**GJR 5 THOMAS KELSO**	**MRC 36**	**GTR 636**	**GTR 392**	11-04	**GTR 2091**	Sc 2-17-25 LM
—	369	9- -80	GJR 6 BELLEVILLE	MRC 37	GTR 637	GTR 393	11-04		Sc 6- -05

CNR 133 was one of two built for the **Grand Junction Railroad.** At amalgamation they became **Midland Railway of Canada** locomotives, and after 1884, part of the **Grand Trunk Railway of Canada** roster.

CNR 134 — 4-4-0 EIGHT-WHEEL TYPE — A-13-a

Cylinder	Gear	Driv.	Pressure	Boiler	T.E.	Haulage	Steam	Stkr.	Weights Drivers/Eng./Total	Water	Fuel	Length	Notes
17x24"	S	63"	140#	ST	13000	13%	sat		49/ 76/ 000	gals	tons	51-0'	

The Portland Company 1880 & 1881 $12,000 — (1) Acquired by CNR 3-01-1923

	Serial	Shipped	New as	1-1884	1898	To	1-1910	Disposition
			—		—	J5	J5	
—	363	5- -80	MRC 12/2	GTR 612	GTR 387	11-04	GTR 2090	Sc 5- -18
—	378	5- -81	MRC 13/2	GTR 613	GTR 388	11-04	GTR 2092	Sc 5- -18
134	379	5-23-81	**MRC 14/2**	**GTR 614**	**GTR 389**	11-04	**GTR 2093**	Sc 6- -25 HQ
—	386	7- -81	MRC 15/2	GTR 615	GTR 390			Sc 9- -04
—	387	8- -81	MRC 16/2	GTR 616	GTR 391	11-04	GTR 2094	Sc 8- -11

CNR 134 was one of five **Midland Railway of Canada** replacements for the first MRC 12-16 which had been sold to the Victoria and the Credit Valley Railways in 1877. With the amalgamation into the **Grand Trunk Railway of Canada**, all became part of the GTR roster.

CNR 135 — 4-4-0 EIGHT-WHEEL TYPE — A-14-a

Cylinder	Gear	Driv.	Pressure	Boiler	T.E.	Haulage	Steam	Stkr.	Weights Drivers/Eng./Total	Water	Fuel	Length	Notes
17x24"	S	69"	140#	ST	13000		sat		47/ 74/129833	1900 gals	8 tons	53-6'	[orig]
17x24"	S	63"	140#	ST	13101	13%	sat		47/ 74/129833	1900 gals	8 tons	53-6'	[CNR]

Rhode Island Locomotive Company 1870 $13,000 — (1) Acquired by CNR 3-01-1923

	Serial	Shipped	New as	1882	nB	1898	1902	11-1904	1-1910	Disposition
			—	—		—	—	J3	J3	
135	246	12-17-70	**GWR 142**	**GTR 777**	1892	**GTR 34**	**GTR 119**	**GTR 292**	**GTR 2123**	Sc 2-05-25 LM

CNR 135 was one of nine standard gauge odd-numbered freight 4-4-0s built for the **Great Western Railway of Canada.** At amalgamation they all became **Grand Trunk Railway of Canada** locomotives. For the complete history of the order, see the entry under CNR A-11-a 129 (page A-13).

CNR 136 — 4-4-0 EIGHT-WHEEL TYPE — A-14-a

Cylinder	Gear	Driv.	Pressure	Boiler	T.E.	Haulage	Steam	Stkr.	Drivers/Eng./Total	Water	Coal	Length	Notes
Specifications							Appliances		Weights	Fuel Capacity		Length	Notes
16x24"	S	66"	#	ST?	00		sat		/ / 000	gals	tons	- '	[orig GWR]
16x24"	S	69"	#	ST	00		sat		/ / 000	gals	tons	- '	[GTR N]
17x24"	S	69"	140#	ST	13000		sat		47/ 74/ 000	gals	tons	53-6'	[GTR J3]
17x24"	S	63"	140#	ST	13101	13%	sat		47/ 74/129833	1900 gals	8 tons	53-6'	[2136,136]

Rhode Island Locomotive Company 1871 $13,000 — (1) Acquired by CNR 3-01-1923

	Serial	Shipped	New as	8-1882	nB	1898	12-1902	11-1904	11-1904	1-1910	Disposition
			—	—		—	—	N	J3	J3	
136	258	4-05-71	**GWR 127**	**GTR 714**		**GTR 513**			**GTR 343**	**GTR 2136**	Sc 3-04-25 LM
—	259	4- -71	GWR 129	GTR 715	12-84	GTR 77	GTR 164		GTR 293	GTR 2134	Sc 10- -20
—	278	5- -71	GWR 131	GTR 716		GTR 149		GTR 149			Sc 11- -04
—	279	6- -71	GWR 133	GTR 717		GTR 514			GTR 348	GTR 2137	Sc 7- -15
—	287	6- -71	GWR 135	GTR 718		GTR 150		GTR 150			Sc 9- -08
—	288	6- -71	GWR 137	GTR 719		GTR 151		GTR 151			Sc 9- -06
—	289	7- -71	GWR 139	GTR 720	6-86	GTR 354			GTR 354		Sc 9- -09
—	290	7- -71	GWR 141	GTR 721		GTR 152		GTR 152			Sc 9- -09

CNR 136 was from an order of eight odd-numbered passenger locomotives built for the **Great Western Railway of Canada.** At amalgamation they became **Grand Trunk Railway of Canada** locomotives. The subsequent increase of cylinder size on four of the batch accounted for the difference in GTR classification in 1904. Driver diameters varied through the service lives as well, particularly the 70-inches on GTR 152 and 63-inches on GTR 2136, the future CNR 136.

Not a large number of former Great Western Railway steamers became CNR stock. What is thought to be **GWR 133**, posed with its crew about 1881 at what is now Highbury Avenue in east London, was in the same builder's lot as CNR 136. Typical of dozens of 4-4-0s delivered from Rhode Island during the early 1870s, it carried some interesting features. An early version of a cross-head water pump was between the drivers. During this period, engines not fitted with driver or engine truck brakes were known by GTR and CNR crews as "barefoots". A Richardson "pop" safety valve was mounted on top of the firebox. The open safety valve had been introduced in 1867, and without a muffler, kicked in with such a startling crack, railroaders were not long before referring to the device as the "pop" valve. Marker lamps and a bell adorn the pilot beam, and a metal "Hiawatha warrior" decorated the top of the kerosene headlight's vent. [CNR PHOTO/HAROLD K. VOLLRATH/WES DENGATE COLLECTION]

CNR 137 — 4-4-0 EIGHT-WHEEL TYPE — A-14-a

Cylinder	Gear	Driv.	Pressure	Boiler	T.E.	Haulage	Steam	Stkr.	Drivers/Eng./Total	Water	Fuel	Length	Notes
Specifications							Appliances		Weights	Fuel Capacity			
16x24"	S	54"	#		00		sat		/ / 000	gals	tons	- '	[orig]
16x24"	S	57"	#	ST	00		sat		/ / 000	gals	tons	- '	[GTR final specs] *(a)*
16x24"	S	62"	#	ST	00		sat		/ / 000	gals	tons	- '	[GTR final specs] *(b)*
16x24"	S	63"	#	ST	00		sat		/ / 000	gals	tons	- '	[GTR final specs] *(c)*
17x24"	S	63"	140#	ST	13101	13%	sat		47/ 74/129833	1900 gals	8 tons	53-6'	[GTR final specs] *(d)*

Rhode Island Locomotive Company 1871-1872 $13,000 (1) Acquired by CNR 3-01-1923

	Serial	Shipped	New as	-1873?	af-1882	??	8-1882	1898	11-1904	1-1910		Disposition	To
			—	—	—	—	—	—	J3	J3			
—	325	11- -71	GWR 170				GTR 791	GTR 155			*a*	Sc 6- -00	
—	326	11- -71	GWR 172				GTR 792	GTR 156			*b*	So 6- -01	RLMC
—	327	11- -71	GWR 174	WRR 5	WRR 1/2	GWR 354	GTR 883	GTR 83			*a*	Sc 8- -00	
—	328	12- -71	GWR 176				GTR 794	GTR 157	GTR 125(N)		*c*	Sc 7- -09	
—	329	12- -71	GWR 178				GTR 795	GTR 288	GTR 300	GTR 2135	*d*	Sc 12- -18	
—	330	12- -71	GWR 180				GTR 796	GTR 351	GTR 351	GTR 2138	*d*	Sc 1- -14	
—	331	12- -71	GWR 182				GTR 797	GTR 158	GTR 126(N)		*c*	Sc 7- -09	
—	332	12- -71	GWR 184				GTR 798	GTR 346	GTR 346			Sc 7- -09	
—	333	12- -71	GWR 186				GTR 799	GTR 159			*a*	Sc 11- -02	
—	334	1- -72	GWR 188				GTR 800	GTR 54			*b*	So 9- -01	BPCo
137	335	12-30-71	**GWR 190**				**GTR 801**	**GTR 510**	**GTR 338**	**GTR 2150**	*d*	Sc 9- -23 MP	
—	336	1- -72	GWR 192				GTR 802	GTR 138	GTR 318(N)		*c*	Sc 10- -08	

CNR 137 was one of twelve standard gauge even-numbered freight locomotives built for the **Great Western Railway of Canada.** At amalgamation they became **Grand Trunk Railway of Canada** 4-4-0s. GWR 174 was sold to the Welland Railway Company, GTR 156 to the Rock Lake Mining Company, and GTR 54 to the Brompton Paper Company.

CNR 138 — 4-4-0 EIGHT-WHEEL TYPE — A-14-a

Cylinder	Gear	Driv.	Pressure	Boiler	T.E.	Haulage	Steam	Stkr.	Drivers/Eng./Total	Water	Fuel	Length	Notes
Specifications							Appliances		Weights	Fuel Capacity			
17x24"	S	54"	#		00		sat		/ / 000	gals	tons	- '	[orig]
16x24"	S	57"	#	ST	00		sat		/ / 000	gals	tons	- '	[GTR final specs] *(a)*
16x24"	S	62"	#	ST	00		sat		/ / 000	gals	tons	- '	[GTR final specs] *(b)*
16x24"	S	63"	#	ST	00		sat		/ / 000	gals	tons	- '	[GTR final specs] *(c)*
17x24"	S	63"	140#	ST	13101	13%	sat		47/ 74/129833	1900 gals	8 tons	53-6'	[GTR final specs] *(d)*

Rhode Island Locomotive Company 1873 $13,000 (1) Acquired by CNR 3-01-1923

	Serial	Shipped	New as	8-1882	1898	12-1902	11-1904	11-1904	1-1910	1-1910		Disposition	To
			—	—	—	—	J3	N	J3	N			
—	555	9- -73	GWR 302	GTR 857	GTR 112						*a*	Sc 11- -02	
—	556	9- -73	GWR 304	GTR 858	GTR 60						*a*	So 8- -02	
—	557	9- -73	GWR 306	GTR 859	GTR 113						*a*	Sc 6- -00	
—	558	9- -73	GWR 308	GTR 860	GTR 68	GTR 155		GTR 121		GTR 1981	*c*	Sc 4- -11	
—	559	9- -73	GWR 310	GTR 861	GTR 501		GTR 332		GTR 2162		*d*	Sc 10- -16	
—	560	9- -73	GWR 312	GTR 862	GTR 84	GTR 170		GTR 136			*c*	Sc 6- -06	
—	561	9- -73	GWR 314	GTR 863	GTR 114			GTR 114			*c*	Sc 6- -06	
138	562	9-20-73	**GWR 316**	**GTR 864**	**GTR 290**		**GTR 290**		**GTR 2155**		*d*	Sc 9- -23 MP	
—	563	9- -73	GWR 318	GTR 865	GTR 74						*b*	So 7- -02	SPCo
—	564	9- -73	GWR 320	GTR 866	GTR 85	GTR 176					*a*	Sc 11- -03	
—	565	10- -73	GWR 322	GTR 867	GTR 115		GTR 291		GTR 2156		*d*	Sc 1- -13	
—	566	10- -73	GWR 324	GTR 868	GTR 502		GTR 333		GTR 2163		*d*	Sc 4- -11	
—	567	10- -73	GWR 326	GTR 869	GTR 36	GTR 120		GTR 120			*c*	Sc 9- -08	
—	568	10- -73	GWR 328	GTR 870	GTR 116						*a*	Sc 9- -00	
—	569	10- -73	GWR 330	GTR 871	GTR 46	GTR 130		GTR 130		GTR 1982	*c*	So 7- -12	NSRN
—	570	10- -73	GWR 332	GTR 872	GTR 81						*b*	Sc 11- -02	
—	571	10- -73	GWR 334	GTR 873	GTR 117						*a*	Sc 5- -00	
—	572	10- -73	GWR 336	GTR 874	GTR 503		GTR 334		GTR 2164		*d*	Sc 11- -13	
—	573	10- -73	GWR 338	GTR 875	GTR 65						*b*	So 4- -02	NPCo
—	574	10- -73	GWR 340	GTR 876	GTR 118						*b*	So 9- -04	
—	575	10- -73	GWR 342	GTR 877	GTR 119						*a*	Sc 11- -00	
—	576	10- -73	GWR 344	GTR 878	GTR 120						*a*	Sc 6- -98	
—	577	10- -73	GWR 346	GTR 879	GTR 504		GTR 355		GTR 2165		*d*	Sc 8- -14	
—	578	10- -73	GWR 348	GTR 880	GTR 25	GTR 107					*b*	Sc 9- -03	
—	579	10- -73	GWR 350	GTR 881	GTR 517		GTR 353		GTR 2167		*d*	Sc 7- -14	

CNR 138 was one of twenty-five built as even-numbered freight locomotives for the **Great Western Railway of Canada.** At amalgamation they became **Grand Trunk Railway of Canada** stock. **CNR 138** (as GTR 864) received a new boiler in 1895. GTR 74 was sold to the Sun Portland Cement Company, GTR 1982 to the North Shore Railway & Navigation Company, and GTR 65 to the National Portland Cement Company.

GTR 333 was in the same builder's lot and GTR class as CNR 138. It had, by the time of the photograph at Lindsay about 1906, lost its rimmed Rhode Island steam and sand domes for ones of GTR's distinctive design. The cab front windows had yet to be shielded from the heat of the firebox and the boxy kerosene headlight replaced by one of the rounded models. The extended smokebox had probably been applied by the GTR during the period of fashionability which had begun in the early 1880s. [W.D. (BILL) THOMSON COLLECTION]

CNR 139-140 — 4-4-0 EIGHT-WHEEL TYPE — A-14-a

Specifications							Appliances		Weights	Fuel Capacity		Length	Notes
Cylinder	Gear	Driv.	Pressure	Boiler	T.E.	Haulage	Steam	Stkr.	Drivers/Eng./Total	Water	Coal		
16x24"	S	54"	#		00		sat		/ / 000	gals	tons	- '	[orig]
16x24"	S	57"	#	ST	00		sat		/ / 000	gals	tons	- '	[GTR final specs] *(a)*
16x24"	S	58"	#	ST	00		sat		/ / 000	gals	tons	- '	[GTR final specs] *(e)*
16x24"	S	62"	#	ST	00		sat		/ / 000	gals	tons	- '	[GTR final specs] *(b)*
16x24"	S	63"	#	ST	00		sat		/ / 000	gals	tons	- '	[GTR final specs] *(c)*
17x24"	S	63"	140#	ST	13000		sat		47/ 74/129833	1900 gals	8 tons	(53-6')	[GTR final specs] *(d)*
17x24"	S	63"	140#	ST	13101	13%	sat		38/ 64/119833	1900 gals	8 tons	(42-10')	[140]

Rhode Island Locomotive Company 1873 $13,000 — (2) Acquired by CNR 3-01-1923

	Serial	Shipped	New as	8-1882	1898	12-1902	11-1904	11-1904	1-1910		Disposition	To
			—	—	—	—	J3	N	J3			
—	491	12- -72	GWR 148	GTR 780	GTR 175			GTR 154		*e*	Sc 6- -06	
—	492	1- -73	GWR 250	GTR 831	GTR 103					*b*	Sc 11- -02	
—	493	3- -73	GWR 252	GTR 832	GTR 23					*b*	Sc 11- -02	
—	494	3- -73	GWR 254	GTR 833	GTR 104					*b*	Sc 8- -99	
—	495	3- -73	GWR 256	GTR 834	GTR 105					*b*	Sc 8- -00	
—	496	3- -73	GWR 258	GTR 835	GTR 352		GTR 352				Sc 9- -08	
—	497	3- -73	GWR 260	GTR 836	GTR 106					*a*	Sc 8- -00	
—	498	3- -73	GWR 262	GTR 837	GTR 24	GTR 106		GTR 112		*c*	Sc 6- -06	
139	499	3-27-73	**GWR 264**	**GTR 838**	**GTR 498**	**GTR 498**	**GTR 329**		**GTR 2160**	*d*	So 3-23-25 LM	
—	500	4- -73	GWR 266	■ GTR 755	GTR 345			GTR 345	GTR 2166	*d*		**CNR 252**
—	501	4- -73	GWR 268	GTR 840	GTR 499		GTR 330		GTR 2161	*d*	Sc 11- -16	
—	502	4- -73	GWR 270	GTR 841	GTR 107					*a*	Sc 9- -00	
—	503	4- -73	GWR 272	GTR 842	GTR 72	GTR 161				*a*	Sc 11- -04	
—	504	4- -73	GWR 274	GTR 843	GTR 58	GTR 144		GTR 144		*e*	Sc 6- -06	
140	508	4-23-73	**GWR 276**	**GTR 844**	**GTR 500**	**GTR 500**	**GTR 331**		**GTR 2169**	*d*	Sc 3-23-25 LM	
—	509	5- -73	GWR 278	GTR 845	GTR 108					*b*	Sc 3- -03	
—	510	5- -73	GWR 280	GTR 846	GTR 64					*a*	Sc 8- -02	
—	511	5- -73	GWR 282	GTR 847	GTR 316		GTR 316		GTR 2158	*d*	Sc 4- -18	
—	512	5- -73	GWR 284	GTR 848	GTR 317		GTR 317		GTR 2159	*d*	Sc 4- -18	
—	513	5- -73	GWR 286	GTR 849	GTR 82	GTR 169		GTR 135		*c*	So 1- -07	A&S
—	514	5- -73	GWR 288	GTR 850	GTR 109			GTR 115		*e*	So 10- -05	PBCo
—	515	5- -73	GWR 290	GTR 851	GTR 110					*a*	Sc 10- -00	
—	516	5- -73	GWR 292	GTR 852	GTR 26	GTR 110		GTR 118		*e*	So 11- -05	QRLP 1
—	517	5- -73	GWR 294	GTR 853	GTR 59					*a*	Sc 3- -03	
—	518	5- -73	GWR 296	GTR 854	GTR 73	GTR 162		GTR 129		*c*	Sc 9- -09	
—	519	5- -73	GWR 298	GTR 855	GTR 111			GTR 111		*e*	Sc 4- -05	
—	520½	5- -73	GWR 300	GTR 856	GTR 78	GTR 167		GTR 134		*e*	So 11- -06	QRLP 4

■ to GWR 209 for passenger service sometime after delivery

CNR 139 and **140** were two of twenty-seven standard gauge even-numbered freight locomotives built for the **Great Western Railway of Canada**. At amalgamation they became part of the **Grand Trunk Railway of Canada** roster.

GTR 135 was sold to the Atlantic & Superior Railway, GTR 115 to the Phoenix Bridge Company, and GTR 118 and 134 to the Quebec Railway Light & Power Company. The serial (boiler) number "520½" for GWR 300 was assigned the locomotive because of a serial sequencing error at Rhode Island.

GT 141 — 4-4-0 EIGHT-WHEEL TYPE — A-14-a

Specifications							Appliances		Weights	Fuel Capacity		Length	Notes
Cylinder	Gear	Driv.	Pressure	Boiler	T.E.	Haulage	Steam	Stkr.	Drivers/Eng./Total	Water	Coal		
17x24"	S	68"	#		00		sat		/ / 000	gals	tons	- '	[orig]
17x24"	S	69"	140#	ST	12000		sat		/ 83/ 000	gals	tons	- '	[rblt] *(a)*
18x26"	S	74½"	140#	ST	13000		sat		/ 99/ 000	gals	tons	- '	[rblt] *(b)*
17x24"	S	63"	150#	ST	14047	14%	sat		47/ 74/129833	1900 gals	8 tons	(42-10')	[141]

Rhode Island Locomotive Company 1874 $13,000 — (1) Acquired by CNR 3-01-1923

	Serial	Shipped	New as	1-1881	1898	10-1899	11-1904	11-1904	1-1910		Disposition	To
			—	—	—	—	H	J3	J3			
—	651	9- -74	GTR 298		GTR 571	GTR 590	GTR 458		GTR 2329 (H)	*b*	Sc 5- -13	
—	652	9- -74	GTR 299		GTR 572	GTR 591	GTR 459		GTR 2330 (H)	*b*	Sc 2- -17	
—	653	9- -74	GTR 300		GTR 420						So 4- -02	MRNS
—	654	9- -74	GTR 301		GTR 421						So 6- -01	MRNS
—	655	9- -74	GTR 302	GTR 320	GTR 321			GTR 321	GTR 2178	*a*	Sc 5- -19	
—	656	9- -74	GTR 303	GTR 313	GTR 431			GTR 327	GTR 2174		Sc 11- -21	
(141)	657	10-01-74	**GTR 304**			**GTR 422**		**GTR 319**	***GT* 2170** (GT)		Sc 10-04-24 DJ	
—	658	10- -74	GTR 305		GTR 423			GTR 320	GTR 2171	*a*	Sc 3- -15	
—	659	10- -74	GTR 306		GTR 424			GTR 325	GTR 2172	*a*	Sc 7- -21	
—	660	10- -74	GTR 307		GTR 425			GTR 326	GTR 2173		So 9- -18	CC&F
—	661	10- -74	GTR 308		GTR 426						Sc 10- -01	
—	662	10- -74	GTR 309		GTR 427						Sc 8- -01	
—	663	10- -74	GTR 310		GTR 428						Sc 10- -01	
—	664	10- -74	GTR 311		GTR 429						Sc 10- -01	
—	665	10- -74	GTR 312		GTR 430						So 7- -01	
—	666	10- -74	GTR 313	GTR 303	GTR 574	GTR 593	GTR 460		GTR 2331 (H)	*b*	So 4- -11	
—	667	10- -74	GTR 314		GTR 432						Sc 9- -01	
—	668	10- -74	GTR 315		GTR 433						Sc 10- -01	
—	669	10- -74	GTR 316		GTR 284			GTR 296	GTR 2176		Sc 11- -15	
—	670	10- -74	GTR 317		GTR 434			GTR 328	GTR 2175		Sc 3- -20	
—	671	10- -74	GTR 318		GTR 285			GTR 297	GTR 2177		So 6- -12	TIR
—	672	11- -74	GTR 319		GTR 435						Sc 9- -01	
—	673	11- -74	GTR 320	GTR 302	GTR 573					*b*	Sc 9- -04	
—	674	11- -74	GTR 321		GTR 436						Sc 9- -01	
—	675	11- -74	GTR 322		GTR 437						Sc 1- -00	

Rhode Island built ninety-seven 4-4-0s with similar specifications for the GWR and GTR between 1871 and 1874, with the last twenty-five being for the GTR. It was likely the new boiler installed in GTR 422 which accounted for its longevity, although not long enough to actually be renumbered to CNR 141. Two fine pre-1923 photographs of the steamer in service on New England lines do exist. **GTR 319** was at Portland, Maine in 1905. [HAROLD K. VOLLRATH/DON McQUEEN COLLECTION]

GT 141 was one of twenty-five built for the **Grand Trunk Railway of Canada. GT 141** (as GTR 422) acquired a new boiler in 1899. GTR 420 and 421 were sold to the Midland Railway Company (of Nova Scotia), GTR 2173 to the Canadian Car & Foundry Company, and GTR 2177 became Thousand Islands Railway 100. Although **141** was taken out-of-service on January 30th 1923, and listed on CNR records as assigned to Portland, Maine, it never received its CNR number as scheduled and was scrapped as GTR 2170 in October 1924.

In 1920 **GTR 2170** was at South Paris, Maine.
[EDWARD L. GREENE PHOTO/CHARLES HOWARD/ DON McQUEEN COLLECTION]

GTW 142-155 — 4-4-0 EIGHT-WHEEL TYPE — A-15-a

Cylinder	Gear	Driv.	Pressure	Boiler	T.E.	Haulage	Steam	Stkr.	Drivers/Eng./Total	Water	Coal	Length	Notes
18x24"	S	63"	150#	ST	16000		sat		58/ 90/165030	2400 gals	7 tons	54-3'	
18x24"	S	63"	150#	ST	15737	16%	sat		58/ 90/165030	2400 gals	7 tons	54-3'	[145-149]
18x24"	S	63"	135#	ST	16000?		sat		58/ 90/165030	2400 gals	7 tons	54-3'	[153-154]

Hinkley was to build thirty-one 4-4-0s for the C&GT during the 1880s, seventeen of which either became GTW locomotives, or were assigned to the US line. **GTR 1098** (152), believed to be at Battle Creek, Michigan soon after being relettered in 1900, had been striped and lettered C&GT 1098 since 1898.
[H.L. GOLDSMITH/GEORGE CARPENTER COLLECTION]
For a view of **GTW 150** a year before retirement in 1925, see Vol. 1, p. 92.

A-14-a A-15-a

Hinkley Locomotive Company	1883	$9000							(6) Acquired by CNR 3-01-1923
	Serial	Shipped	New as	1898	11-1900	To	1-1910	Tender	Disposition
			—	—	—	H2	H2	Tank to	
—	1622	9- -83	C&GT 1	C&GT 1079	*GTW* 1079	11-04	*GTW* 2250		Sc 12- -19 UB
142	1623	9- -83	**C&GT 2**	**C&GT 1080**	***GTW* 1080**	11-04	***GTW* 2251**		Sc 11- -23 UB
(143)	1624	9- -83	**C&GT 3**	**C&GT 1081**	***GTW* 1081**	11-04	***GTW* 2252**		Sc 5- -23 UB
(144)	1625	9- -83	**C&GT 4**	**C&GT 1082**	***GTW* 1082**	11-04	***GTW* 2253**		Sc 4- -23 UB
145	1626	9- -83	**C&GT 5**	**C&GT 1083**	***GTW* 1083**	11-04	***GTW* 2254**		Sc 5-07-27 UB
—	1627	9- -83	C&GT 6*	C&GT 1084	*GTW* 1084	11-04	*GTW* 2255		Sc 1- -20 UB
—	1628	9- -83	C&GT 7	C&GT 1085	*GTW* 1085	11-04	*GTW* 2256		Sc 8- -20 UB
—	1629	9- -83	C&GT 8	C&GT 1086	*GTW* 1086	11-04	*GTW* 2257		Sc 2- -23 UB
146	1630	9- -83	**C&GT 9**	**C&GT 1087**	***GTW* 1087**	11-04	***GTW* 2258**		Sc 4-30-26 UB
147	1631	10- -83	**C&GT 10**	**C&GT 1088**	***GTW* 1088**	11-04	***GTW* 2259**		Sc 8- -25 UB
148	1632	10- -83	**C&GT 11**	**C&GT 1089**	***GTW* 1089**	11-04	***GTW* 2260**		Sc 7-27-26 UB
—	1633	10- -83	C&GT 12	C&GT 1090	*GTW* 1090	11-04	*GTW* 2261		Sc 1- -20 UB
—	1634	10- -83	C&GT 13	C&GT 1091	*GTW* 1091	11-04	*GTW* 2262		Sc 12- -19 UB
149	1635	10- -83	**C&GT 14**	**C&GT 1092**	***GTW* 1092**	11-04	***GTW* 2263**		Sc 3-31-27 UB
—	1636	10- -83	C&GT 15	C&GT 1093	*GTW* 1093	11-04	*GTW* 2264		Sc 12- -19 UB
150	1637	10- -83	**C&GT 16**	**C&GT 1094**	***GTW* 1094**	11-04	***GTW* 2265**		Sc 9- -25 UB
—	1638	10- -83	C&GT 17	C&GT 1095	*GTW* 1095	11-04	*GTW* 2266		Sc 2- -23 UB
—	1639	10- -83	C&GT 18	C&GT 1096	*GTW* 1096	11-04	*GTW* 2267		Sc 12- -19 UB
151	1640	10- -83	**C&GT 19**	**C&GT 1097**	***GTW* 1097**	11-04	***GTW* 2268**		Sc 4-30-26 UB
152	1641	10- -83	**C&GT 20**	**C&GT 1098**	***GTW* 1098**	11-04	***GTW* 2269**		Sc 8-09-26 UB
—	1642	10- -83	C&GT 21	C&GT 1099	*GTW* 1099	11-04	*GTW* 2270		Sc 8- -20 UB
—	1643	11- -83	C&GT 22	C&GT 1100	*GTW* 1100	11-04	*GTW* 2271		Sc 5- -20 UB
153	1644	11- -83	**C&GT 23**	**C&GT 1101**	***GTW* 1101**	11-04	***GTW* 2272**		Sc 10- -25 UB
154	1645	11- -83	**C&GT 24**	**C&GT 1102**	***GTW* 1102**	11-04	***GTW* 2273**	OCS	Sc 3- -24 UB
155	1646	11- -83	**C&GT 25**	**C&GT 1103**	***GTW* 1103**	11-04	***GTW* 2274**		Sc 6-12-25 UB

GTW 142-155 were fourteen of twenty-five built for the **Chicago & Grand Trunk Railroad.** In 1900 they all retained their assignments on **Grand Trunk's** ***western lines (GTW).*** Those remaining in service after 1923 were renumbered and relettered for the **Grand Trunk Western Railway Company.** In 1924 the tender tank of 154 was held for another (unstated) use.

GTW 156-158 — 4-4-0 EIGHT-WHEEL TYPE — A-15-b

Cylinder	Gear	Driv.	Pressure	Boiler	T.E.	Haulage	Steam	Stkr.	Weights Drivers/Eng./Total	Fuel Capacity Water	Coal	Length	Notes
18x24"	S	63"	160#	ST	17000		sat		58/ 90/165030	2400 gals	7 tons	54-3'	

(Specifications: Cylinder–Haulage; Appliances: Steam, Stkr.)

Hinkley Locomotive Company	1889	$9000						(3) Acquired by CNR 3-01-1923
	Serial	Shipped	New as	1898	11-1900	To	1-1910	Disposition
			—	—	—	H2	H2	
(156)	1798	-89	**C&GT 125**	**C&GT 1113**	***GTW* 1113**	11-04	***GTW* 2275**	Sc 6- -23 UB
—	1799	-89	C&GT 126	C&GT 1114	*GTW* 1114	11-04	*GTW* 2276	Sc 2- -23 UB
(157)	1800	-89	**C&GT 127**	**C&GT 1115**	***GTW* 1115**	11-04	***GTW* 2277**	Sc 5- -23 UB
158	1801	-89	**C&GT 129**	**C&GT 1116**	***GTW* 1116**	11-04	***GTW* 2278**	Sc 5- -25 UB
—	1802	-89	C&GT 130*	C&GT 1117	*GTW* 1117	11-04	*GTW* 2279	Sc 1- -20 UB
—	1803	-89	C&GT 131	C&GT 1118	*GTW* 1118	11-04	*GTW* 2280	Sc 12- -19 UB

GTW 156-158 were three of six built for the **Chicago & Grand Trunk Railroad.** In 1900 they remained assigned to **Grand Trunk's** ***western lines (GTW).*** Only one of the four remaining in service after 1923 was renumbered and relettered for the **Grand Trunk Western Railway Company.**

GTW 159-160 — 4-4-0 EIGHT-WHEEL TYPE — A-15-c

Cylinder	Gear	Driv.	Pressure	Boiler	T.E.	Haulage	Steam	Stkr.	Drivers/Eng./Total	Water	Coal	Length	Notes
Specifications							Appliances		Weights	Fuel Capacity			
18x24"	S	69"	160#	ST	15000		sat		/ 98/ 000	gals	tons	- '	[orig]
18x24"	S	63"	140#	ST	15000		sat		65/ 98/190566	2800 gals	10 tons	56-8'	[rblt] *(a)*
18x24"	S	63"	160#	ST	16786	16%	sat		65/ 98/190566	2800 gals	10 tons	56-8'	[160] *(b)*

Unknown Rebuilt by Chicago & Grand Trunk – Fort Gratiot 1888-1892 $8000 (2) Acquired by CNR 3-01-1923

	Serial	Shipped	New as	18??	Rebuilt	1898	11-1900	To	1-1910	Rblt	Disposition	To
			??	—		—	—	H2	H2			
—	??	-??	??	C&GT 26	-88	C&GT 1105	*GTW* 1105	11-04	*GTW* 2282		Sc 5- -20 UB	
—	??	-??	??	C&GT 27	-85	C&GT 1104	*GTW* 1104	11-04	*GTW* 2281	*a*	Sc 11- -22 UB	
159	??	-??	??	**C&GT 28**	-88	**C&GT 1106**	***GTW* 1106**	11-04	***GTW* 2283**	*a*	Sc 8- -23 UB	
—	??	-??	??	C&GT 30	-88	C&GT 1107	*GTW* 1107	11-04	*GTW* 2284		Sc 12- -19 UB	
—	??	-??	??	C&GT 31	-88	C&GT 1108	*GTW* 1108	11-04	*GTW* 2285		Sc 1- -20 UB	
—	??	-??	??	C&GT 32	-88	C&GT 1109	*GTW* 1109	11-04	*GTW* 2286			**CNR 263**
—	??	-??	??	C&GT 68	-90	C&GT 1119	*GTW* 1119	11-04	*GTW* 2290			**GTW 264**
—	??	-??	??	C&GT 70	-91	C&GT 1130	*GTW* 1130	11-04	*GTW* 2294			**GTW 267**
—	??	-??	??	C&GT 98	-92	C&GT 1199	*GTW* 1199	11-04	*GTW* 2295			**GTW 268**
160	??	-??	??	**C&GT 123**	-89	**C&GT 1111**	***GTW* 1111**	11-04	***GTW* 2288**	*b*	Sc 5-12-27 UB	
—	??	-??	??	C&GT 124	-88	C&GT 1112	*GTW* 1112	11-04	*GTW* 2289	*a*	Sc 12- -19 UB	
—	??	-??	??	C&GT 128	-88	C&GT 1110	*GTW* 1110	11-04	*GTW* 2287		Sc 1- -20 UB	

GTW 159 and 160 were from a group of twelve 4-4-0s whose builder and early identities were not recorded by the C&GT. They were apparently rebuilt by the **Chicago & Grand Trunk Railroad** between the years 1885 and 1892 and listed as new locomotives. In 1900 they remained assigned to **Grand Trunk's *western lines (GTW)***. After 1923 the pair with 63-inch drivers was renumbered and relettered for the **Grand Trunk Western Railway Company**. Four from this group with larger drivers were assigned to the B-12-a class.

GTW 161-165 — 4-4-0 EIGHT-WHEEL TYPE — A-15-c

Cylinder	Gear	Driv.	Pressure	Boiler	T.E.	Haulage	Steam	Stkr.	Drivers/Eng./Total	Water	Coal	Length	Notes
Specifications							Appliances		Weights	Fuel Capacity			
18x24"	S	63"	160#	ST	16786	17%	sat		65/ 98/190566	2800 gals	10 tons	56-8'	[CNR]
18x24"	S	68"	160#	ST	17000		sat		/ / 000	gals	tons	56-8'	[rblt] *(b)*

GTR 2299 at Owosso, Michigan in 1912 was a late-in-life representative of the ten built by Brooks for C&GT in 1890. It was still equipped with a kerosene headlight and marker lamps, a tender with flared wooden letterboards, but modified with a steel-plated cab, a cross-compound air pump on the running board, and crescent-shaped driver counterbalance weights.
[H.L. GOLDSMITH/GEORGE CARPENTER COLLECTION]

Brooks Locomotive Company 1890 (359) $8000 — (5) Acquired by CNR 3-01-1923

	Serial	Shipped	New as	1898	11-1900	To	1-1910	Rblt	Disposition
			—	—	—	H2	H2		
161	1619	2- -90	**C&GT 132***	**C&GT 1120**	***GTW* 1120**	11-04	***GTW* 2297**		Sc 3-31-27 UB
162	1620	2- -90	**C&GT 133**	**C&GT 1121**	***GTW* 1121**	11-04	***GTW* 2298**		Sc 6-02-26 UB
—	1621	2- -90	C&GT 134	C&GT 1122	*GTW* 1122	11-04	*GTW* 2299		Sc 12- -22 UB
—	1622	2- -90	C&GT 135	C&GT 1123	*GTW* 1123	11-04	*GTW* 2300		Sc 5- -20 UB
—	1623	2- -90	C&GT 136	C&GT 1124	*GTW* 1124	11-04	*GTW* 2301		Sc 1- -20 UB
163	1624	2- -90	**C&GT 137**	**C&GT 1125**	***GTW* 1125**	11-04	***GTW* 2302**		Sc 8- -23 UB
164	1625	2- -90	**C&GT 138**	**C&GT 1126**	***GTW* 1126**	11-04	***GTW* 2303**		Sc 9- -25 UB
165	1626	2- -90	**C&GT 139**	**C&GT 1127**	***GTW* 1127**	11-04	***GTW* 2304**		Sc 6-02-26 UB
—	1627	2- -90	C&GT 140*	C&GT 1128	*GTW* 1128	11-04	*GTW* 2305	*b*	Sc 8- -22 UB
—	1628	2- -90	C&GT 141	C&GT 1129	*GTW* 1129	11-04	*GTW* 2306	*b*	Sc 1- -21 UB

GTW 161-165 were five of ten built during January 1890 for the **Chicago & Grand Trunk Railroad.** Their assignments did not change after 1900 when the C&GT was incorporated into **Grand Trunk's** *western lines (GTW).* Those still in service after 1923 were renumbered and relettered for the **Grand Trunk Western Railway Company.**

GTW 166-167 — 4-4-0 EIGHT-WHEEL TYPE — A-15-c

Specifications							Appliances		Weights	Fuel Capacity		Length	Notes
Cylinder	Gear	Driv.	Pressure	Boiler	T.E.	Haulage	Steam	Stkr.	Drivers/Eng./Total	Water	Coal		
18x24"	S	63"	160#	ST	17000		sat		65/ 98/190566	2800 gals	10 tons	66-6'	

Rogers Locomotive Works 1891 $9500 — (2) Acquired by CNR 3-01-1923

	Serial	Shipped	New as	1898	11-1900	To	1-1910	Disposition
			—	—	—	H2	H2	
—	4451	1- -91	C&GT 142	C&GT 1131	*GTW* 1131	11-04	*GTW* 2307	Sc 1- -20 UB
—	4452	1- -91	C&GT 143	C&GT 1132	*GTW* 1132	11-04	*GTW* 2308	Sc 1- -20 UB
—	4453	1- -91	C&GT 144	C&GT 1133	*GTW* 1133	11-04	*GTW* 2309	Sc 1- -20 UB
—	4454	1- -91	C&GT 145	C&GT 1134	*GTW* 1134	11-04	*GTW* 2310	Sc 9- -18 UB
166	4459	2- -91	**C&GT 146**	**C&GT 1135**	***GTW* 1135**	11-04	***GTW* 2311**	Sc 8- -23 UB
—	4460	2- -91	C&GT 147	C&GT 1136	*GTW* 1136	11-04	*GTW* 2312	Sc 8- -20 UB
—	4461	2- -91	C&GT 148	C&GT 1137	*GTW* 1137	11-04	*GTW* 2313	Sc 12- -20 UB
—	4462	2- -91	C&GT 149	C&GT 1138	*GTW* 1138	11-04	*GTW* 2314	Sc 1- -20 UB
(167)	4468	2- -91	**C&GT 150**	**C&GT 1139**	***GTW* 1139**	11-04	***GTW* 2315**	Sc 5- -23 UB
—	4469	2- -91	C&GT 151	C&GT 1140	*GTW* 1140	11-04	*GTW* 2316	Sc 8- -20 UB

GTW 166 and 167 were two of ten built for the **Chicago & Grand Trunk Railroad.** All remained on **Grand Trunk's** *western lines (GTW)* after 1900. After nationalization in 1923, two may have been still in service but only one was renumbered and relettered for the **Grand Trunk Western Railway Company.**

GTW, GT 168-172 — 4-4-0 EIGHT-WHEEL TYPE — A-16-a

Specifications							Appliances		Weights	Fuel Capacity		Length	Notes
Cylinder	Gear	Driv.	Pressure	Boiler	T.E.	Haulage	Steam	Stkr.	Drivers/Eng./Total	Water	Coal		
18x24"	S	73"	185#	ST	20000		sat		/ / 000	gals	tons	61-3'	[orig]
18x24"	S	63"	175#	ST	18360	18%	sat		89/127/236820	3700 gals	8 tons	61-3'	[rblt]

Cooke Locomotive & Machine Company 1893 $9777 — (5) Acquired by CNR 3-01-1923

	Serial	Shipped	New as	1898	11-1900	To	1-1910	Disposition	To
			—	—	—	H3	H3		
168	2281	7- -93	**C&GT 154**	**C&GT 1141**	***GTW* 1141**	11-04	***GTW* 2317**	Sc 8-21-23 G	**L&M**
—	2282	7- -93	C&GT 155*	C&GT 1142	*GTW* 1142	11-04	*GTW* 2318	Sc 5- -20 UB	
(169)	2283	7- -93	**C&GT 156**	**C&GT 1143**	***GTW* 1143**	11-04	***GTW* 2319**	Sc 4- -23 UB	
(170)	2284	7- -93	**C&GT 157**	**C&GT 1144**	***GTW* 1144**	11-04	***GT* 2320 (GT)**	Sc 5- -23 UB	
171	2285	7- -93	**C&GT 158**	**C&GT 1145**	***GTW* 1145**	11-04	***GT* 2321 (GT)**	Sc 11- -23 UB	
—	2286	7- -93	C&GT 159	C&GT 1146	*GTW* 1146	11-04	*GTW* 2322	Sc 2- -23 UB	
—	2287	8- -93	C&GT 160	C&GT 1147	*GTW* 1147	11-04	*GTW* 2323	Sc 12- -19 UB	
—	2288	8- -93	C&GT 161	C&GT 1148	*GTW* 1148	11-04	*GTW* 2324	Sc 11- -22 UB	
—	2289	9- -93	C&GT 162*	C&GT 1149	*GTW* 1149	11-04	*GTW* 2325	Sc 12- -22 UB	
—	2290	9- -93	C&GT 163	C&GT 1150	*GTW* 1150	11-04	*GTW* 2326	Sc 12- -19 UB	
172	2291	9- -93	**C&GT 164**	**C&GT 1151**	***GTW* 1151**	11-04	***GTW* 2327**	Sc 8- -23 UB	
—	2292	9- -93	C&GT 165	C&GT 1152	*GTW* 1152	11-04	*GTW* 2328	Sc 11- -22 UB	

Sitting outside the hazy train shed of Chicago's Dearborn Station in July 1908, **GTR 1150** was right at home in the age of coal smoke and exhaust steam. [HAROLD K. VOLLRATH/WES DENGATE COLLECTION]

GTW and **GT 168-172** were five of twelve passenger locomotives built for the **Chicago & Grand Trunk Railroad.** After consolidation in 1900, all but two remained assigned to **Grand Trunk's** *western lines (GTW).* Those still in service after 1923 were renumbered and relettered for the **Grand Trunk Western Railway Company.** The 2320 and 2321 were transferred to New England lines about 1910. These two 4-4-0s, assigned to Portland, and scheduled to become GT 170 and 171, were cut up in May 1923 as GTR 2320 and 2321. ***GTW* 168** was sold to **Lennore & McIlvenna**, of Detroit, Michigan for $3000, but its final disposition is unknown.

In the cleaner air of small-town Michigan sometime after 1910, two crew members are typically hard at work shifting coal towards the tender gates of **GTR 2321** (171). Although both steamers still relied on kerosene for lighting, they had been upgraded with steel-plated cabs, crescent-shaped driving wheel counterweights and slotted Janney couplers to accommodate pin-and-link equipment. [AL PATERSON COLLECTION]

173-199 **Numbers not used**

CONTENTS

B CLASS: 212-399

THIS SECTION

CNR 212-399

B CLASS
4-4-0 EIGHT-WHEEL TYPE

Class "B" was assigned road numbers **200-399** for American (Standard) or Eight-Wheel Types with drivers more than 63 inches. The class, totalling 185 locomotives, came from four predecessor roads: eighty-four from the **Grand Trunk Railway of Canada** – sixteen of which were assigned GTW and GT lines; seventy-five from the **Grand Trunk Pacific Railway** (ten of which had been sold to the CaNoR but not renumbered until 1923); twenty-one from the **Canadian Government Railway**, and four from the **Canadian Northern Railway**.

In 1919 the road number allotment pattern assigned **212-215** to CaNoR 4-4-0s, and **216-236** to those of the CGR. In 1920 the GTP 4-4-0s (including the CaNoR sales) were assigned **324-399**, and in 1923 the GTR-GTW 4-4-0s were numbered **240-323**.

Although the distribution of the B class sub-series assigned by the CNR Motive Power Department in 1919 may appear to be lacking sequential order, it should be noted the class was built around CaNoR classes still in use. CaNoR vacancies were reused to classify CGR and GTR motive power both in 1919 and 1923 respectively. The practice continued for other stock acquired after 1924. These reassigned CaNoR classes are listed in Part Two: *CNR Class Summary*. All dates are mm-dd-yr.

200-211

Numbers not used

CNR 212 — 4-4-0 EIGHT-WHEEL TYPE — B-1-a

Specifications							Appliances		Weights	Fuel Capacity		Length	Notes
Cylinder	Gear	Driv.	Pressure	Boiler	T.E.	Haulage	Steam	Stkr.	Drivers/Eng./Total	Water	Coal		
17x24"	S	66"	140#		12500	12%	sat		54/ 86/166000	3600 gals	tons	- '	[CaNoR 1909]

Canadian Locomotive & Engine Company (Dübs) 1889 — (1) Acquired by CNR 9-01-1919

	Serial	Shipped	New as	8-1901	1-1912	Disposition
			—	—	B-1-A	
212	383	7-26-89	**NP&M 7**	**CaNoR 44**	**CaNoR 61**	Sc 7-29-20 PK
—	384	7-29-89	NP&M 8	CaNoR 45	CaNoR 62	Sc bf -19

CNR 212 was one of two 4-4-0s built for the **Northern Pacific & Manitoba Railway** which in 1901 was incorporated into the **Canadian Northern Railway**.

CNR 213 — 4-4-0 EIGHT-WHEEL TYPE — B-2-a

Specifications							Appliances		Weights	Fuel Capacity		Length	Notes
Cylinder	Gear	Driv.	Pressure	Boiler	T.E.	Haulage	Steam	Stkr.	Drivers/Eng./Total	Water	Coal		
18x26"	S	69"	150#		14368	13%	sat		62/ 98/ 000	gals	tons	- '	[CaNoR 1909]

Rhode Island Locomotive Company 1885 — (1) Acquired by CNR 9-01-1919

	Serial	Shipped	New as	1887	1898	1900	5-1902	1-1912	Disposition
			—	—	—	—	—	B-2-A	
213	1554	6- -85	**CB 2**	**ATSF 504**	**ATSF 293**	**ATSF 89**	**CaNoR 48/2**	**CaNoR 63**	Sc 7-26-20 PK

CNR 213 was built for the **Reasor Balanced Slide Valve Company** and lettered **Cooper Bros.** It was then sold to the **Atchison Topeka & Santa Fe Railroad**. It was resold to the **Canadian Northern Railway** via the Chicago second-hand dealer **James T. Gardiner**.

CNR 214 — 4-4-0 EIGHT-WHEEL TYPE — B-3-a

Specifications							Appliances		Weights	Fuel Capacity		Length	Notes
Cylinder	Gear	Driv.	Pressure	Boiler	T.E.	Haulage	Steam	Stkr.	Drivers/Eng./Total	Water	Coal		
18x24"	S	70"	#		00		sat		/ / 000	gals	tons	- '	[ATSF]
18x24"	S	69"	150#		14368	14%	sat		66/101/191000	3600 gals	8 tons	- '	[CaNoR 1909]
18x24"	S	69"	160#	WT	15360	17%	H-C		66/101/191000	4500 gals	8 tons	56-9'	[CNR]

Schenectady Locomotive Works 1888 $4500 — (1) Acquired by CNR 9-01-1919

	Serial	Shipped	New as	1898	1900	5-1902	1-1912	New boiler	Superheated	Disposition
	(2180	1- -87)	—	—	—	—	B-3-A			
214	2388	1- -88	**ATSF 601**	**ATSF 249**	**ATSF 49**	**CaNoR 49/2**	**CaNoR 64**	-13 PK	2-14 PK	Sc 5-29-36 MQ

In service for its third owner, **214** was at London on May 28th 1927, nine years before retirement. Boiler replacement, installed in 1913, no doubt explained its service longevity, and would account for the numerous improvements to appliances. Besides being superheated and converted to a dynamo-generated electrical system, other upgrades included hanging steps on steel running boards and blanked forward side windows when the cab was steel plated. During the 1930s, the 4-4-0 would acquire a boiler tube pilot and tender wafer. [JOHN D. KNOWLES COLLECTION]

CNR 214 was one of twenty-one locomotives built for the **Atchison Topeka & Santa Fe Railroad** as **597-617** (#2384-2404) between September 1887 and January 1888. The Schenectady serial (boiler) number 2388 was used for **ATSF 49**, but the *CNR Mechanical Department Locomotive Diagrams* B-3-a sheet gives the serial number and build-date for **214** as 2180 – the number originally was assigned to ATSF 52 in 1887. Rather than an error in documentation, railway historians believe the two locomotives switched boilers at some time before ATSF 49 became a **Canadian Northern Railway** locomotive bought through the Chicago second-hand dealer **James T. Gardiner.** This could explain why CaNoR records show the build-date as 1887 for 2180, while the documents from Schenectady have August 1888 for 2388. **CaNoR 64** (CNR 214) was rebuilt with a new boiler at Winnipeg.

CNR 215 — 4-4-0 EIGHT-WHEEL TYPE — B-4-a

Specifications							Appliances		Weights	Fuel Capacity		Length	Notes
Cylinder	Gear	Driv.	Pressure	Boiler	T.E.	Haulage	Steam	Stkr.	Drivers/Eng./Total	Water	Coal		
18x24"	S	70"	#		00		sat		/ / 000	gals	tons	- '	[ATSF]
17½x24"	S	68"	150#		13781	14%	sat		67/100/ 000	3700 gals	tons	- '	[CaNoR 1909]
17x24"	S	69"	150#		13000	13%	sat		67/100/ 000	gals	tons	- '	[CNR]

Manchester Locomotive Company 1888 — (1) Acquired by CNR 9-01-1919

	Serial	Shipped	New as	1898	1900	5-1902	1-1912	Disposition
			—	—	—	—	B-4-A	
215	1338	1- -88	**ATSF 633**	**ATSF 322**	**ATSF 103**	**CaNoR 50**/2	**CaNoR 65**	Sc 7-29-20 PK

CNR 215 was one of ten built for the **Atchison Topeka & Santa Fe Railroad** as **633-642** (#1338-1347) during January and February 1888. They were renumbered to **ATSF 325-330** in 1898 and again to **ATSF 106-111** in 1900. ATSF 103 (**215**) was purchased by the **Canadian Northern Railway** through the Chicago second-hand dealer **James T. Gardiner.**

CNR 216-220 — 4-4-0 EIGHT-WHEEL TYPE — B-5-a

Cylinder	Gear	Driv.	Pressure	Boiler	T.E.	Haulage	Steam	Stkr.	Drivers/Eng./Total	Water	Coal	Length	Notes
Specifications							Appliances		Weights	Fuel Capacity			
18x24"	S	69"	140#		13000		sat		80/ / 000	gals	tons	- '	[orig]
17x24"	S	69"	170#	BEL	14365		sat		71/110/195550	3500 gals	7 tons	55-2'	[216,219,220 by 1917]
17x24"	S	69"	170#	BEL	14620	14%	sat		71/110/195550	3500 gals	7 tons	54-8'	[219 by 1921]
17x24"	S	69"	180#		15160		sat		71/110/195550	3500 gals	7 tons	55-2'	[218,220 by 1917]

Canadian Locomotive & Engine Company 1883-1884 (C-14) — (5) Acquired by CNR 9-01-1919

	Serial	Shipped	New as	Rebuilt	1-1912		12-1915		Disposition	To
			—	nB	D3 145%		A3 70%			
—	273	4- -83	IRC 146						Wr 3- -87	
216	274	4- -83	**IRC 147**	5-95 BEL	**IRC 1083**		**CGR 1083**		Sc 5-05-20 AK	
—	275	4- -83	IRC 148	1-96	IRC 1089	(D21)	CGR 1089	(A3-21)		**CNR 223**
—	276	4- -83	IRC 149	11-96	IRC 1090	(D21)	CGR 1090	(A3-21)		**CNR 224**
—	277	4- -83	IRC 150	9-96	IRC 1091	(D21)	CGR 1091	(A3-21)		**CNR 225**
—	278	1- -84	IRC 151	—	IRC 1105	(D14)			Rs by -14	
217	279	?1- -84	**IRC 152**	9-95	**IRC 1084**		**CGR 1084**		Sc 3- -20 AK	
—	280	?1- -84	IRC 153	11-95	IRC 1088	(D3A)	CGR 1088	(A3-3A)		**CNR 221**
218	281	?2- -84	**IRC 154**	12-94	**IRC 1085**		**CGR 1085**		Sc 7-30-20 AK	
219	282	?2- -84	**IRC 155**	8-94 BEL	**IRC 1086**		**CGR 1086**		Sc 7- -22 AK	
—	283	?2- -84	IRC 156	2-97	IRC 1092	(D21)	CGR 1092	(A3-21)		**CNR 226**
—	284	3- -84	IRC 157	—	IRC 1106	(D14)			Rs by -14	
—	285	3- -84	IRC 158	—	IRC 1107	(D14)		Rs by -14	So -17	CC&F
—	286	3- -84	IRC 159	10-98	IRC 1096	(D14A)	CGR 1096	(A3-14A)		**CNR 230**
—	287	3- -84	IRC 160	—					Wr 3- -87	
—	288	3- -84	IRC 161	12-97	IRC 1095	(D)	CGR 1095	(A3)		**CNR 229**
(220)	289	3- -84	**IRC 162**	10-94 BEL	**IRC 1087**		**CGR 1087**		Sc 9- -21 AK	
—	290	?4-08-84	IRC 163	6-96	IRC 1093	(D21)	CGR 1093	(A3-21)		**CNR 227**
—	291	?4- -84	IRC 164	3-96	IRC 1094	(D21)	CGR 1094	(A3-21)		**CNR 228**

CNR 216-221 and **223-230** were from nineteen 4-4-0s built under contract C-14 for the **Intercolonial Railway of Canada**. Between 1894 and 1897, at Moncton shops, fourteen from the group received extensively rebuilding which included the installation of new boilers. During the rebuilding, three, IRC 147, 155 and 162 (**216, 219** and **220**), received new boilers with Belpaire fireboxes. In

(text continues on next page)

Twenty-three years after leaving Kingston, IRC 1st 162 (220) at Petitcodiac, New Brunswick in 1908, was assigned the Saint John to Moncton passenger express. The Belpaire firebox and enlarged steam chest were part of the locomotive's rebuild at IRC's Moncton shops in October 1894. At the time of the photograph, the 4-4-0 was running with only one marker lamp, mounted on the left-hand side of the smokebox.
[TED MCQUINN/DON MCQUEEN COLLECTION]

December 1895 IRC 154 (**218**) had its boiler exchanged with IRC 137 {Fleming 4-4-0 #29 of 2-1883}. The reboilered locomotives became IRC 1083-1096 in 1912, and, after 1919, B-5 **216-221** and **223-230**. CGR 1086 (**219**) was held for sale to the Kent Northern Railway, but as the sale was never consummated, the steamer went to scrap.

The three which did not receive new boilers became IRC D14 1105-1107 and were taken out-of-service by the **Canadian Government Railways** prior to October 1914, and disposed of before 1917. CGR 1107 was sold for scrap to the Canadian Car & Foundry Company.

CNR 221 — 4-4-0 EIGHT-WHEEL TYPE — B-5-b

Cylinder	Gear	Driv.	Pressure	Boiler	T.E.	Haulage	Steam	Stkr.	Drivers/Eng./Total	Water	Coal	Length	Notes
Specifications							*Appliances*		*Weights*	*Fuel Capacity*			
18x24"	S	69"	140#		13000		sat		80/ / 000	gals	tons	- '	[orig]
18x24"	S	69"	180#	BEL	17750	17%	sat		71/110/181000	3900 gals	7 tons	55-2'	[af. 1895]

Canadian Locomotive & Engine Company 1884 (C-14) — (1) Acquired by CNR 9-01-1919

	Serial	Shipped	New as	Rebuilt	1-1912	12-1915	Disposition
			—	nB	D3^A 172%	A3-3^A 85%	
221	280	?1- -84	**IRC 153**	11-95 BEL	**IRC 1088**	**CGR 1088**	Sc 2- -23 BA

CNR 221 was built for the **Intercolonial Railway of Canada**. The complete history is under CNR 216-220 (page B-4).

CNR 222 — 4-4-0 EIGHT-WHEEL TYPE — B-5-b

Cylinder	Gear	Driv.	Pressure	Boiler	T.E.	Haulage	Steam	Stkr.	Drivers/Eng./Total	Water	Coal	Length	Notes
Specifications							*Appliances*		*Weights*	*Fuel Capacity*			
17x24"	S	60"	130#		00		sat		/ / 000	gals	tons	- '	[orig]
17x24"	S	63"	160#		15000		sat		59/ 88/166500	2500 gals	5 tons	50-7'	[by 1917]

Hinkley Locomotive Company 1880 — (1) Acquired by CNR 9-01-1919

	Serial	Shipped	New as	c.1882	Rebuilt	1-1912		12-1915	af. 8-01-1914	Disposition	To
			—	—	—	D8^A 137%		A2-8^A 70%	A1		
—	—	5-18-80	IRC 7/3		?10-97	IRC 1051	(D8)			So by -16	B-PCC
—	—	5- -80	IRC 32/3*	NB&PEI 2					CGR 1175	Sc -18	
—	—	5- -80	IRC 35/3							Sc by -23	
(222)	—	5- -80	**IRC 39**/2		1-98	**IRC 1099**		**CGR 1099**		Sc 12-31-20 PU	

CNR 222 was the last of four built for the **Intercolonial Railway of Canada** with no assigned builder's serial numbers. It was rebuilt by IRC Moncton either in December 1897 or January 1898. It went to scrap as a **Canadian Government Railways** 4-4-0, assigned to the National Transcontinental Railway.

IRC 1051 was sold sometime between 1914 and 1915 to By-Products Coke Co. as number 1. IRC 32 was sold to the New Brunswick & Prince Edward Island Railway as number 2, only to return to the CGR with the sale of NB&PEI on August 1st 1914. It was condemned on December 18th 1917 and dismantled in 1918.

CNR 223-228 — 4-4-0 EIGHT-WHEEL TYPE — B-5-c

Cylinder	Gear	Driv.	Pressure	Boiler	T.E.	Haulage	Steam	Stkr.	Drivers/Eng./Total	Water	Coal	Length	Notes
Specifications							*Appliances*		*Weights*	*Fuel Capacity*			
18x24"	S	69"	140#		13000		sat		80/ / 000	gals	tons	- '	[orig]
17x24"	S	69"	160#	EWT	13475		sat		71/110/195550	3500 gals	7 tons	54-8'	[224,228 by 1917]
17x24"	S	69"	170#	EWT	14365	14%	sat		71/110/195550	3500 gals	7 tons	55-2'	[CNR]

Canadian Locomotive & Engine Company 1883-1884 (C-14) — (6) Acquired by CNR 9-01-1919

	Serial	Shipped	New as	Rebuilt	1-1912	12-1915	Disposition
			—	nB	D21 145%	A3-21 70%	
(223)	275	4- -83	**IRC 148**	1-96	**IRC 1089**	**CGR 1089**	Sc 1- -22 AK
(224)	276	4- -83	**IRC 149**	11-96	**IRC 1090**	**CGR 1090**	Sc 10-21-20 PU
(225)	277	4- -83	**IRC 150**	9-96	**IRC 1091**	**CGR 1091**	Sc 1- -22 AK
226	283	?2- -84	**IRC 156**	2-97	**IRC 1092**	**CGR 1092**	Sc 5-05-20 AK
227	290	?4-08-84	**IRC 163**	6-96	**IRC 1093**	**CGR 1093**	Sc 5-25-21 AK
228	291	?4- -84	**IRC 164**	3-96	**IRC 1094**	**CGR 1094**	Sc 10- -22 EH

CNR 223-228 were part of an order for the **Intercolonial Railway of Canada**. The complete history is under CNR 216-220 (page B-4).

CNR 229 — 4-4-0 EIGHT-WHEEL TYPE — B-5-d

Cylinder	Gear	Driv.	Pressure	Boiler	T.E.	Haulage	Steam	Stkr.	Drivers/Eng./Total	Water	Coal	Length	Notes
17x24"	S	69"	180#		14000		sat		/110/ 000	gals	tons	45-6'	
17x24"	S	69"	180#		15000	15%	sat		71/110/181000	2700 gals	5 tons	54-4'	[by 1917]

Canadian Locomotive & Engine Company 1884 (C-14) — (1) Acquired by CNR 9-01-1919

CNR	Serial	Shipped	New as	Rebuilt	1-1912	12-1915	Disposition
			—	nB	D(odd) 154%	A3 70%	
229	288	3- -84	**IRC 161**	12-97	**IRC 1095**	**CGR 1095**	Sc 5-05-20 AK

CNR 229 was built for the **Intercolonial Railway of Canada.** The complete history is under CNR 216-220 (page B-4).

CNR 230 — 4-4-0 EIGHT-WHEEL TYPE — B-5-e

Cylinder	Gear	Driv.	Pressure	Boiler	T.E.	Haulage	Steam	Stkr.	Drivers/Eng./Total	Water	Coal	Length	Notes
18x24"	S	69"	170#		16000	16%	sat		71/110/195550	3500 gals	7 tons	54-4'	[by 1917]
18x24"	S	69"	170#	EWT	16380	16%	sat		71/110/195550	3500 gals	7 tons	55-2'	[CNR]

Canadian Locomotive & Engine Company 1884 (C-14) — (1) Acquired by CNR 9-01-1919

CNR	Serial	Shipped	New as	Rebuilt	1-1912	12-1915	Disposition
			—	nB	D14^{A} 162%	A3-14 80%	
230	286	3- -84	**IRC 159**	10-1898	**IRC 1096**	**CGR 1096**	Sc 6- -22 AK

CNR 230 was built for the **Intercolonial Railway of Canada.** The complete history is under CNR 216-220 (page B-4).

CNR 231-232 — 4-4-0 EIGHT-WHEEL TYPE — B-6-a

Cylinder	Gear	Driv.	Pressure	Boiler	T.E.	Haulage	Steam	Stkr.	Drivers/Eng./Total	Water	Coal	Length	Notes
17¼x24"	S	69"	160#	EWT	14000	14%	sat		55/ 91/165700	3100 gals	6 tons	52-10'	[CGR,CNR]

Manchester Locomotive Company 1888 — (2) Acquired by CNR 9-01-1919

CNR	Serial	Shipped	New as	1-1912	12-1915		Disposition	To
			—	D23 138%	A3-23 70%			
231	1372?	3- -88	**IRC 197**	**IRC 1100**	**CGR 1100**		Sc 2- -23 AK	
—	1370?	3- -88	IRC 198	IRC 1101	CGR 1101	Rs 12-18-17	So -23 AK	HAC
232	1371?	3- -88	**IRC 199**	**IRC 1102**	**CGR 1102**		Sc 10- -21 AK	
—	1373?	3- -88	IRC 200	IRC 1103	CGR 1103		So 5-01-18 AK	QOR 8

CNR 231 and 232 were from four 4-4-0s apparently ordered by the **Atchison Topeka & Santa Fe Railroad,** but which were purchased by the **Intercolonial Railway of Canada.** Manchester records are incomplete as to the assigned serial numbers; the best evidence suggests the IRC road numbers were sequenced as shown above. CGR 1101, although condemned by the **Canadian Government Railways** was sold to H.A. Carson, a contractor. CGR 1103 was sold to the Quebec Oriental Railway. The final disposition of either of the 4-4-0s is unknown.

CNR 233-235 — 4-4-0 EIGHT-WHEEL TYPE — B-7-a

Cylinder	Gear	Driv.	Pressure	Boiler	T.E.	Haulage	Steam	Stkr.	Drivers/Eng./Total	Water	Coal	Length	Notes
16x24"	S	66"	#		00		sat		/ / 000	gals	tons	- '	[orig]
16x24"	S	69"	160#	EWT	12000		sat		58/ 90/150000	3000 gals	6 tons	50-0'	[by 1917]
16x24"	S	69"	160#	EWT	12160	12%	sat		58/ 90/150000	2800 gals	6 tons	50-6'	[CNR]

Manchester Locomotive Company 1875 — (3) Acquired by CNR 9-01-1919

CNR	Serial	Shipped	New as	Rebuilt	1-1912		12-1915	Disposition	To
			—		D17 121%		A2-17 60%		
233	684	6- -75	**IRC 55/2**	6-96	**IRC 1108**		**CGR 1108**	Sc 10- -20 AK	
—	685	6- -75	IRC 56/2	-89				So -10 AK	CRY 35
—	686	6- -75	IRC 57/2					Sc bf -10	
—	687	6- -75	IRC 58/2	8-97	IRC 1109		CGR 1109	So 12-18-17 AK	HAC
—	688	6- -75	IRC 59/2	-97				Sc -10	
—	689	6- -75	IRC 60/2					Sc bf -12	
—	690	6- -75	IRC 61/2	5-97 C				Sc -03	
—	691	6- -75	IRC 62/2	6-94	IRC 1116	(D16^{A})	CGR 1116	Sc by 10-14	
234	692	6- -75	**IRC 63/2**	12-96	**IRC 1110**		**CGR 1110**	Sc 6-14-20 AK	
235	695	6- -75	**IRC 66/2**	3-96	**IRC 1111**		**CGR 1111**	Sc 7- -23 AK	

C: Cleveland Uniflow Cylinders

When **IRC** 2nd **66** (235) arrived in Moncton during June 1875, the last of the order merited a photograph, and it appears that several employees were invited to help record the event. Most of the as-built amenities would be improved or discarded during the half-century the Manchester eight-wheeler was in service. By the end of the century the vertical stave pilot would go the way of the pin-and-link coupling, the diamond stack would be replaced by a straight blast pipe, splasher covers over the drivers would be discarded, and the arched side windows of the wooden cab would be squared and the forward ones blanked. An early victim of decor was the ornate painting on the side of the kerosene headlight, as it too would be replaced by newer models, and dropped to the centre of the smokebox. [W.D. (BILL) THOMSON COLLECTION]

CNR 233-235 were the only remaining 4-4-0s from the ten built for the **Intercolonial Railway of Canada.** They were built between February and April 1875 and likely delivered during June. IRC 2nd 59 was the first company locomotive to have Cleveland Uniflow cylinders installed. See Appendix BB for more information. Most were rebuilt at the Moncton shops. **Canadian Government Railways 1108** was condemned on September 8th 1919 but became **CNR 233. CNR 235** was scheduled to be scrapped in July 1923, but was not dismantled until November 1924.

IRC 56 was sold to the Caraquet Railway. CGR 1109 was condemned December 18th 1917 and sold in 1918 to contractor H.A. Carson. Its final disposition is unknown.

CNR 236 — 4-4-0 EIGHT-WHEEL TYPE — B-8-a

Specifications							Appliances		Weights	Fuel Capacity		Length	Notes
Cylinder	Gear	Driv.	Pressure	Boiler	T.E.	Haulage	Steam	Stkr.	Drivers/Eng./Total	Water	Coal		
16x24"	S	63"	#		00		sat		/ / 000	gals	tons	- '	[CPR: 6-7]
16x24"	S	51"	#		00		sat		/ / 000	gals	tons	- '	[CPR: 8-9]
17x24"	S	69"	160#	EWT	14000	14%	sat		56/ 85/140350	1800 gals	5 tons	50-6'	[CGR, CNR]

Baldwin Locomotive Works – Burnham, Parry, Williams & Company 1884 $10,000 (1) Acquired by CNR 9-01-1919

	Serial	Shipped	New as	7-1886	8-1887	1-1912		12-1915	Tender to	Disposition	To
			—	—	—	D2 137%		A2-2 70%			
236	7273	4- -84	**Mills-CPR 6 NICOLA**	**GofC**	**IRC 184**	**IRC 1119**		**CGR 1119**	**CN 50157**	Sc 3- -25 AK	
—	7274	4- -84	Mills-CPR 7 KAMLOOPS	GofC	IRC 185	IRC 1078	D2^A			Sc by 10-14 AK	
—	7498	11- -84	Mills-CPR 8 SHUSWAP	GofC	IRC 186	IRC 1079	D2^A			So -15 AK	K&C
—	7501	11- -84	Mills-CPR 9 COLUMBIA	GofC	IRC 187	IRC 1080	D2^B			Sc by 10-14 AK	

CNR 236 was one of four 4-4-0s which, although built for the syndicate **D.O. Mills & Company**, were lettered **Canadian Pacific Railway.** The federal government stipulated that all the construction equipment engaged in building the new railway was to be so lettered, and to be turned over to the operator, the Canadian Pacific Railway *Company* (incorporated in 1881) after the contractors had finished building their sections of the line. However, in July 1886 the CPR refused to purchase any of the nine locomotives used by **Andrew Onderdonk** to construct the Pacific section of the railway and the federal government placed them in storage. In August 1888, eight of the nine were transferred to the **Intercolonial Railway of Canada.** (For more details, see Lavallée: *Canadian Pacific Steam Locomotives* pp. 366-375 and Berton: *The National Dream* pp. 268*ff*). The four Baldwins were repaired and altered by Fleming & Son, Saint John, New Brunswick, and placed in IRC service during 1888. **IRC 184** was again rebuilt in 1900 at the Moncton shops.

IRC 1079 was retired by October 1914 and sold to Kirk & Cook, contractors for the Saint John Valley Railway as 51(?). It was scrapped by the company in 1920. The tender of **236**, renumbered to **CN 50157**, was assigned to Atlantic Region 15-ton crane 50157 (Browning 1911) and retired for scrap in 1933.

237-239 Numbers not used

CNR 240-243 4-4-0 EIGHT-WHEEL TYPE B-9-a

Cylinder	Gear	Driv.	Pressure	Boiler	T.E.	Haulage	Steam	Stkr.	Weights Drivers/Eng./Total	Fuel Capacity Water	Coal	Length	Notes
16x24"	S	66"	135#		00		sat		/ / 000	gals	tons	- '	[orig GTR 280-293]
16x24"	S	60"	135#		00		sat		/ / 000	gals	tons	- '	[orig GTR 294-297]
17x24"	S	69"	150#	ST	13000		sat		52/ 83/ 000	gals	tons	54-0'=55-0'	[nB 1884-1891]
17x24"	S	69"	150#	WT	13000	13%	sat		56/ 86/ 000	gals	tons	51-3'=55-2'	[nB 1894-1898]

Schenectady Locomotive Works 1873 $13,000 — (4) Acquired by CNR 3-01-1923

	Serial	Shipped	New as	nB	1898	11-1904	1-1910	1913	Leased	Disposition	To
			—		—	J1	J1	Lengths	B-9-a		
243	910	8- -73	**GTR 280**	8-94	**GTR 301**	**GTR 224**	**GTR 2008**	54-8'		Sc 12- -24 LM	
—	911	8- -73	GTR 281	-95	GTR 292	GTR 223	GTR 2007	51-3'		Sc 12- -18 MP	
—	920	9- -73	GTR 282	-98	GTR 336	GTR 227	GTR 2011	55-2'		Sc 11-23-16	
240	922	9- -73	**GTR 283**	4-89	**GTR 337**	**GTR 228**	**GTR 1998**	54-0'		Sc 12- -24 LM	
—	928	10- -73	GTR 284	-96	GTR 282	GTR 221	GTR 2005	54-9'		So 4- -18	TIR 101
—	929	10- -73	GTR 285	-94	GTR 302	GTR 225	GTR 2009	51-10'		Sc 4- -18	
—	937	11- -73	GTR 286*	-96	GTR 283	GTR 222	GTR 2006	54-9'		Sc 7- -16	
—	939	11- -73	GTR 287	-94	GTR 303	GTR 226	GTR 2010	51-6'		Sc 4- -18	
—	941	11- -73	GTR 288	11-84	GTR 364	GTR 233	GTR 2002	55-0'		Sc 7- -19	
—	942	11- -73	GTR 289	-89	GTR 338	GTR 229	GTR 1999	55-0'		Sc 5- -21	
242	950	12- -73	**GTR 290**	5-86	**GTR 353**	**GTR 231**	**GTR 2001**	54-0'		So 2- -25 C	**TIR 102**
241	951	12- -73	**GTR 291**	8-89	**GTR 339**	**GTR 230**	**GTR 2000**	55-0'	**TIR** 2-25	So 6- -26 C	**TIR 241**
—	952	12- -73	GTR 292	8-84	GTR 365	GTR 234	GTR 2003	55-0'		Sc 9- -19	
—	953	12- -73	GTR 293		GTR 505	GTR 237	GTR 2013	54-0'		Sc 5- -15	
—	954	12- -73	GTR 294		GTR 506					So 3- -03	LIMCo
—	955	12- -73	GTR 295	9-84	GTR 366	GTR 235	GTR 2004	55-0'		Sc 7-08-16	
—	956	1- -74	GTR 296	-98	GTR 415	GTR 236	GTR 2012	54-0'		Sc 6- -18	
—	957	1- -74	GTR 297	3-85	GTR 358	GTR 232				Sc 6- -06	

Two representatives of the future B-9-a class, photographed in action about five years apart, had undergone several fundamental changes. **GTR 292**, about to roll through a cattle guard in a pastoral Clarkson, Ontario about 1898, still had pin-and-link coupling, a vertical stave pilot and diamond stack.
[DETAIL: AL PATERSON COLLECTION]

Given the pristine condition and freshly graphited smokebox of **GTR 505** at Glencoe about 1903, the consist is likely to be more a business car than a pay car. The style of domes on both 4-4-0s was a clue to other technical upgrades. The torpedo-shape pair on the boiler of 292 were acquired during a 1884 rebuilding to newer GTR standards, whereas 505 retained the as-built style of the builder.
[PHOTO DETAIL: CNR PHOTO 48439/GORD SOUTTER COLLECTION]

Another pair of representatives of the B-9-a class had been rebuilt with extended smokeboxes sporting GTR's unique shape of domes in 1894 and 1896 respectively. **GTR 302** with "13" painted on the lens of the headlight was in District 13 on the former N&NW between Burlington Crossing and Allandale about 1898. [DON McQUEEN COLLECTION]

CNR 240-243 were four of thirteen passenger and five freight 4-4-0s built for the **Grand Trunk Railway of Canada. CNR 241** was initially authorized for scrapping on January 19th 1925, but was repaired instead and rented to the **Thousand Islands Railway** as **241**, beginning in February 1925. It was finally sold to the TIR in June 1926 for $3300 to supplant TIR 102 (CNR 242). **TIR 241** was replaced by CNR 44 (4-4-2T GTR 2-1892) and scrapped in December 1927. **CNR 242** was sold to the **TIR** as **102** for $3300 to replace TIR 101 (ex GTR 2005) which had been in TIR service since 1918. **TIR 102**, damaged in a 1926 fire and replaced by **271**, was returned to CNR for scrapping in December 1927, but not placed on CNR records. GTR 506 was sold to the London Iron Metal Company.

B-9-a

GTR 2005, with its bell in full revolution, was probably photographed along the Toronto Esplanade before its transfer in 1918 to the TIR. [AL PATERSON COLLECTION]

CNR 244-245 — 4-4-0 EIGHT-WHEEL TYPE — B-9-b

Specifications							Appliances		Weights	Fuel Capacity		Length	Notes
Cylinder	Gear	Driv.	Pressure	Boiler	T.E.	Haulage	Steam	Stkr.	Drivers/Eng./Total	Water	Coal		
17x24"	S	69"	155#	WT	13244	13%	sat		50/ 76/132000	2500 gals	7 tons	45-1'	[CNR]

Baldwin Locomotive Works - Burnham, Parry, Williams & Company 1886 $8500 (2) Acquired by CNR 3-01-1923

	Serial	Shipped	New as	8-1899	1-1905	1-1910	Rear pilot	Disposition
			—	—	J1	J1		
244	8285	12- -86	**CAR 13**	**GTR 608**	**GTR 1320**	**GTR 2119**	12-21	Sc 6- -25 HQ
245	8287	12- -86	**CAR 14**	**GTR 609**	**GTR 1321**	**GTR 2120**		Sc 6- -25 HQ

CNR 244-247 were from two Baldwin orders for the **Canada Atlantic Railway**. All four came to the CNR via the **Grand Trunk Railway of Canada.**

Gracefully appointed CAR 15 (246) with its trimmed driving wheel spokes and tender decor was in Ottawa's Elgin Street yard about 1895. [WILLIAM J. TOPLEY PHOTO/PAC C-6317]
It was likely posed for the photographer as there was no coal in the tender, nor any evidence of smoke or leaking steam. Well-worn and utilitarian GTR 2119 (244) was likely in the Montreal scrap line about 1925. [*CNR LOCOMOTIVE DATA CARD*] The introduction of automatic couplers at the turn of the century dictated the change in pilot design. When converted to electricity, the steam dome directly above the firebox prevented the dynamo from being located above the firebox ahead of the cab. Placed into a non-standard location between the domes, it had to be fitted with an extra-long exhaust pipe.

B-9-b

CNR 246-247 — 4-4-0 EIGHT-WHEEL TYPE — B-9-b

Specifications							Appliances		Weights	Fuel Capacity		Length	Notes
Cylinder	Gear	Driv.	Pressure	Boiler	T.E.	Haulage	Steam	Stkr.	Drivers/Eng./Total	Water	Coal		
17x24"	S	69"	155#	WT	13244	13%	sat		50/ 76/132000	2500 gals	7 tons	45-1'	[CNR]

Baldwin Locomotive Works – Burnham, Parry, Williams & Company 1888 $9000 (2) Acquired by CNR 3-01-1923

	Serial	Shipped	New as	8-1899	1-1905	1-1910	Disposition
			—	—	—	—	
246	9005	1- -88	**CAR 15**	**GTR 610**	**GTR 1322**	**GTR 2121**	Sc 12-27-24 HQ
247	9130	1- -88	**CAR 16**	**GTR 611**	**GTR 1323**	**GTR 2122**	Sc 11-15-24 HQ

CNR **246** and **247**. See the note under 244-245 (page B-10).

CNR "247" — 0-6-0T SADDLE TANK SWITCHER TYPE — O-8-a

History is under CNR O-8-a **7101** (page O-21).

CNR 248-249 — 4-4-0 EIGHT-WHEEL TYPE — B-10-a

Specifications							Appliances		Weights	Fuel Capacity		Length	Notes
Cylinder	Gear	Driv.	Pressure	Boiler	T.E.	Haulage	Steam	Stkr.	Drivers/Eng./Total	Water	Coal		
16x24"	S	66"	#		00		sat		/ / 000	gals	tons	- '	[orig]
17x24"	S	69"	140#	ST	11902	12%	sat		47/ 74/129883	1900 gals	8 tons	53-6'	[2125/248]
17x24"	S	70"	140#	ST	11791	12%	sat		47/ 74/129883	1900 gals	8 tons	54-8'	[2126/249]

Rhode Island Locomotive Company 1870 GTR installed new boilers (nB) 1885-1893 $13,000 (2) Acquired by CNR 3-01-1923

	Serial	Shipped	New as	8-1882	nB	1898	11-1904	11-1904	1-1910	Mods	Disposition
			—	—		—	J3	N	J3		
—	234	12- -70	GWR 113	GTR 707							Wr 2- -88
—	235	12- -70	GWR 115	GTR 708		GTR 172		GTR 142			Sc 6- -06
249	236	12-05-70	**GWR 117**	**GTR 709**	-93	**GTR 313**	**GTR 313**		**GTR 2129**		Sc 3-05-25 LM
—	237	12- -70	GWR 119	GTR 710	10-85	GTR 359	GTR 302		GTR 2124		Sc 1- -16
—	238	12- -70	GWR 121	GTR 711	7-94	GTR 305	GTR 305		GTR 2127		Sc 3- -19
248	239	12-05-70	**GWR 123**	**GTR 712**	11-85	**GTR 360**	**GTR 303**		**GTR 2125**	p	Sc 9- -25 LM
—	240	12- -70	GWR 125	GTR 713		GTR 516	GTR 350		GTR 2133		Sc 5- -19

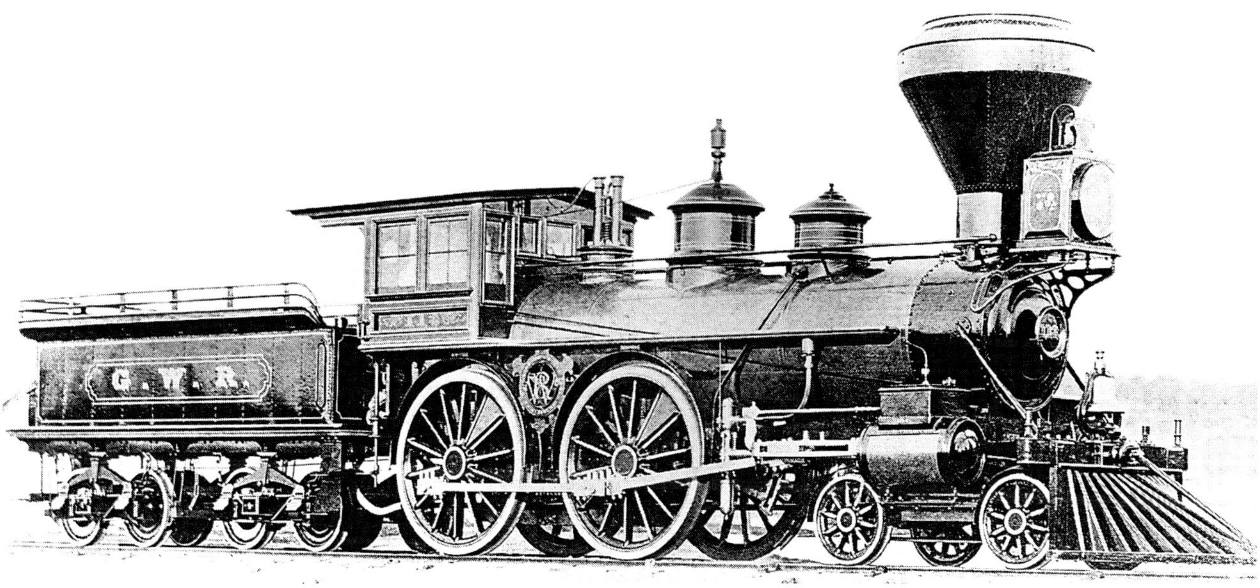

CNR **248** and **249** were two of seven standard gauge 4-4-0s built for the **Great Western Railway of Canada** as odd-numbered passenger locomotives. At amalgamation they became **Grand Trunk Railway of Canada** locomotives. A rear pilot (p) was installed on **248** (as GTR 2129) in December 1921.

The five 4-4-0s which eventually became CNR's B-10-a class had come from three years of Rhode Island production. Another pair which had been rebuilt with different specifications found their way into the A-14-a class. As built, balloon-stacked **GWR 113** at Providence in December 1870, sported both the earliest version of the Richardson safety valve atop the firebox and an elaborate builder's plate between the drivers. [RHODE ISLAND LOCOMOTIVE CO. PHOTO/H.L. GOLDSMITH/ GEORGE CARPENTER COLLECTION]

CNR 250-251 — 4-4-0 EIGHT-WHEEL TYPE — B-10-a

Cylinder	Gear	Driv.	Pressure	Boiler	T.E.	Haulage	Steam	Stkr.	Drivers/Eng./Total	Water	Coal	Length	Notes
Specifications							Appliances		Weights	Fuel Capacity			
16x22"	S	66"	#		00		sat		/ / 000	gals	tons	- '	[orig]
17x24"	S	69"	140#	ST	11902	12%	sat		47/ 74/129883	1900 gals	8 tons	53-6'	[CNR]

Rhode Island Locomotive Company 1872 GTR installed new boilers (nB) 1884-1893 $13,000 (2) Acquired by CNR 3-01-1923

	Serial	Shipped	New as	8-1882	nB	1898	11-1904	1-1910	Disposition
			—	—		—	J3	J3	
—	433	9- -70	GWR 189	GTR 745		GTR 508	GTR 336	GTR 2148	Sc 6- -14
251	434	9-30-72	**GWR 191**	**GTR 746**	8-84	**GTR 367**	**GTR 309**	**GTR 2143**	Sc 5-13-25 LM
—	435	10- -72	GWR 193	GTR 747		GTR 509	GTR 337	GTR 2149	Sc 4- -18
—	436	10- -72	GWR 195	GTR 748	8-84	GTR 368	GTR 310	GTR 2144	Sc 5- -21
—	437	10- -72	GWR 197	GTR 749	6-88	GTR 344	GTR 344	GTR 2153	Sc 2- -14
—	438	10- -72	GWR 199	GTR 750	-93	GTR 314	GTR 314	GTR 2145	Sc 9-30-14
—	439	11- -72	GWR 201	GTR 751	10-86	GTR 355	GTR 355	GTR 2154	Sc 1- -16
(250)	440	10-28-72	**GWR 203**	**GTR 752**	1-95	**GTR 286**	**GTR 298**	**GTR 2139**	Sc 4- -23 MP

CNR 250 and 251 were two of eight standard gauge 4-4-0s built for the **Great Western Railway of Canada** as odd-numbered passenger locomotives. At amalgamation they became **Grand Trunk Railway of Canada** locomotives.

CNR 252 — 4-4-0 EIGHT-WHEEL TYPE — B-10-a

Cylinder	Gear	Driv.	Pressure	Boiler	T.E.	Haulage	Steam	Stkr.	Drivers/Eng./Total	Water	Coal	Length	Notes
Specifications							Appliances		Weights	Fuel Capacity			
16x24"	S	54"	#		00		sat		/ / 000	gals	tons	- '	[orig]
17x24"	S	70"	140#	ST	11791	12%	sat		47/ 74/129883	1900 gals	8 tons	53-6'	[2166/252]

Rhode Island Locomotive Company 1873 $13,000 (1) Acquired by CNR 3-01-1923

	Serial	Shipped	New as	c-1873?	8-1882	nB	1898	11-1904	1-1910	Disposition
			—	—	—		—	J3	J3	
251	500	3-27-73	**GWR 266**	**GWR 209**	**GTR 755**	9-88	**GTR 345**	**GTR 345**	**GTR 2166**	Sc 3-11-25 LM

CNR 252 was one of twenty-seven odd-numbered standard gauge 4-4-0s built for freight service on the **Great Western Railway of Canada**. At amalgamation the group became **Grand Trunk Railway of Canada** 4-4-0s. See the entry under CNR 4-4-0 139 and 140 for the complete history of the order (page A-18). At some unknown date GWR 266 was renumbered to GWR 209 when its drivers were changed from freight to passenger service diameter.

GTR J3 **2166** (252), at the "Big Shop" in Stratford about 1923, had undergone a boiler change, had its lighting system converted to electricity and drivers counterbalanced with crescent-shaped weights. However, the use of four-paned cab windows seemed to have endured throughout a half-century of service.
[AL PATERSON COLLECTION]

GTW 253-260 — 4-4-0 EIGHT-WHEEL TYPE — B-11-a

Specifications							Appliances		Weights	Fuel Capacity		Length	Notes
Cylinder	Gear	Driv.	Pressure	Boiler	T.E.	Haulage	Steam	Stkr.	Drivers/Eng./Total	Water	Coal		
18x24"	S	72"	#		00		sat		/ / 000	gals	tons	- '	[orig]
17x24"	S	73"	160#	ST	13000		sat		65/104/ 000	gals	tons	57-6'	[2179]
18x24"	S	73"	160#	ST	14487	14%	sat		65/104/177550	3000 gals	8 tons	*a:* 56-2' *b:* 57-6'	

Rhode Island Locomotive Company 1882 $9000? — (8) Acquired by CNR 3-01-1923

	Serial	Shipped	New as	Rebuilt	1898	1900	To	1-1910	*OL*	Disposition	To
			—	—	—	—	H2	H2			
255	1209	9- -82	**C&GT 57***		**C&GT 1071**	***GTW* 1071**	11-04	***GTW* 2242**	*a*	Sc 3-31-27 UB	
253	1210	9- -82	**C&GT 58**	12-97	**C&GT 1069**	***GTW* 1069**	11-04	***GTW* 2179**	*b*	Sc 3-31-27 UB	
256	1211	9- -82	**C&GT 59**		**C&GT 1072**	***GTW* 1072**	11-04	***GTW* 2243**	*a*	Sc 4-20-28 UB	
257	1212	9- -82	**C&GT 60**		**C&GT 1073**	***GTW* 1073**	11-04	***GTW* 2244**	*a*	Sc 4-20-28 UB	
258	1213	9- -82	**C&GT 61**		**C&GT 1074**	***GTW* 1074**	11-04	***GTW* 2245**	*b*	Sc 12-19-30 UB	
259	1214	9- -82	**C&GT 62**		**C&GT 1075**	***GTW* 1075**	11-04	***GTW* 2246**	*a*	Sc 11-10-27 UB	
260	1215	9- -82	**C&GT 63**		**C&GT 1076**	***GTW* 1076**	11-04	***GTW* 2247**	*b*	Sc 4-14-27 UB	
—	1216	9- -82	C&GT 64		C&GT 1077	*GTW* 1077	11-04	*GTW* 2248			**GT 261**
—	1217	9- -82	C&GT 65		C&GT 1078	*GTW* 1078	11-04	*GTW* 2249			**GT 262**
254	1218	9- -82	**C&GT 66**	12-97	**C&GT 1070**	***GTW* 1070**	11-04	***GTW* 2241**	*b*	Sc 9-10-27 UB	

GTW 253-262 were built for the **Chicago & Grand Trunk Railroad**, and remained on **Grand Trunk's *western lines (GTW)*** after 1900. All were renumbered and relettered **Grand Trunk Western** after 1923. In 1897 C&GT 58 and 66 (**253** and **254**) were rebuilt to 17x24" 13%, but later converted back to 18x24" 14%.

All of the ten locomotives built by Rhode Island in 1882 remained in US service until retirement between 1927 and 1930, including the pair transferred to New England lines in 1920. **GTW 259**, in the scrap line at Battle Creek in 1927, had a number of "betterments" (as railway records referred to capital improvements). Some of these installed after 1915 included an electric headlight, tender marker lamps, footholds and tender handrails and a two-piece stack. The sign "Held For Disposition" on the boiler below the bell may have indicated the possibility of an interested buyer. [*CNR LOCOMOTIVE DATA CARD*]

GT 261-262 — 4-4-0 EIGHT-WHEEL TYPE — B-11-a

Specifications							Appliances		Weights	Fuel Capacity		Length	Notes
Cylinder	Gear	Driv.	Pressure	Boiler	T.E.	Haulage	Steam	Stkr.	Drivers/Eng./Total	Water	Coal		
18x24"	S	72"	160#	ST	14000		sat		65/104/177550	3000 gals	8 tons	56-2'	[orig]
18x24"	S	73"	150#	ST	13581	13%	sat		65/104/177550	3000 gals	8 tons	56-2'	[CNR]

Rhode Island Locomotive Company 1882 $9000 — (2) Acquired by CNR 3-01-1923

	Serial	Shipped	New as	1898	1900	To	1-1910	9-07-1920	To		Disposition
			—	—	—	H2	H2	H2	B-11-a		
261	1216	9- -82	**C&GT 64**	**C&GT 1077**	***GTW* 1077**	11-04	***GTW* 2248**	***GT* 2248**	**GT 261**	2-23-24	Sc 7-01-27 DJ
262	1217	9- -82	**C&GT 65**	**C&GT 1078**	***GTW* 1078**	11-04	***GTW* 2249**	***GT* 2249**	**GT 262**	4-05-24	Sc 7-01-27 DJ

GT 261 and 262 were built as part of an order for the **Chicago & Grand Trunk Railroad.** See the entry under GTW 253-260 for the complete history of the order (above). Although the pair remained on **Grand Trunk's *western lines (GTW)*** after 1900, they were sold to the New England lines (*GT*) in 1920 for $5000. At nationalization they were relettered and renumbered as **Grand Trunk** locomotives, and remained in New England service.

GTW 263-264 — 4-4-0 EIGHT-WHEEL TYPE — B-12-a

Specifications							Appliances		Weights	Fuel Capacity		Length	Notes
Cylinder	Gear	Driv.	Pressure	Boiler	T.E.	Haulage	Steam	Stkr.	Drivers/Eng./Total	Water	Coal		
18x24"	S	69"	160#	ST	15327	15%	sat		65/ 98/190566	2800 gals	10 tons	56-8'	

Unknown — Rebuilt by Chicago & Grand Trunk – Fort Gratiot 1888 & 1890 — (2) Acquired by CNR 3-01-1923

	Serial	Shipped	New as	1888	Rebuilt	1898	1900	To	1-1910	Disposition
			—	—		—	—	H2	H2	
263	??	-??	??	**C&GT 32**	-88	**C&GT 1109**	***GTW* 1109**	11-04	***GTW* 2286**	Sc 5-20-25 UB
264	??	-??	??	**C&GT 68**	-90	**C&GT 1119**	***GTW* 1119**	11-04	***GTW* 2290**	Sc 11-28-27 UB

Two views of future B-12-a 4-4-0s contrast rural and urban settings. Two chickens blurred their movement as the birds scurried out of the path of a passenger train headed by GTR 2286 (263) as it eased to a stop at an unidentified Michigan station about 1915. [AL PATERSON COLLECTION]

The complete history of the order(s) for **263** and **264** is under GTW A-15-c 159-160 (page A-22).

GTW 265-266 — 4-4-0 EIGHT-WHEEL TYPE — B-12-a

Specifications							Appliances		Weights	Fuel Capacity		Length	Notes
Cylinder	Gear	Driv.	Pressure	Boiler	T.E.	Haulage	Steam	Stkr.	Drivers/Eng./Total	Water	Coal		
16x20"	S	60"	#		00		sat		/ 51/ 000	gals	tons	- '	[265 orig]
16x20"	S	66"	#		00		sat		/ 51/ 000	gals	tons	- '	[266 orig]
18x24"	S	69"	160#	ST	15327	15%	sat		65/ 98/190566	2800 gals	10 tons	56-8'	[Rblt]

The Portland Company 1857 — Rebuilt by Chicago & Grand Trunk – Fort Gratiot 1890 & 1891 — (2) Acquired by CNR 3-01-1923

	Serial	Shipped	New as	1873 (t)	1874 (f)	SG	10-1885	Rblt	1898	1900	11-1904	1-1910	Disposition
			—	—	—		—		—	—	H2	H2	
265	87	1- -57	**GTR 165 POWNAL**	**GTR 128**	**GTR 434**	7-75	**GTR 495**	1890	**DGHM 559**	***GTW* 559**	***GTW* 1062**	***GTW* 2292**	Sc 4-01-27 UB
266	88	1- -57	**GTR 166 J.B. BROWN**	**GTR 136**	**GTR 435**	5-75	**GTR 496**	1891	**DGHM 560**	***GTW* 560**	***GTW* 1063**	***GTW* 2293**	Sc 9-10-26 UB

GTW **265** and **266** were a pair of broad gauge 4-4-0s built in 1857 for the **Grand Trunk Railway of Canada** – one each for freight and passenger service. Both received interim (t) road numbers in 1873 and final (f) ones by 1874. They were standard-gauged (SG) in 1875. In 1898 they were assigned to the **Detroit Grand Haven & Milwaukee Railroad**, and after amalgamation remained on **Grand Trunk's** *western lines (GTW)*.

The movement of a crew member in front of **GTR 2292** (265) at the impressive Durand depot in 1908 also resulted in a blur. The 2292 was one of two of the oldest 4-4-0s to see service after nationalization. The first phase of their career was from 1857 to 1890-91. During their second lease on life they were hand-me-downs to the GTR-controlled DG&M in 1898. [L.A. WHYTE/WES DENGATE COLLECTION]

GTW 267-268 — 4-4-0 EIGHT-WHEEL TYPE — B-12-a

Cylinder	Gear	Driv.	Pressure	Boiler	T.E.	Haulage	Steam	Stkr.	Drivers/Eng./Total	Water	Coal	Length	Notes
Specifications							Appliances		Weights	Fuel Capacity		Length	Notes
12&20x24"	S	"	#		00		sat		/ / 000	gals	tons	- '	[4-4-0C in 1898]
18x24"	S	69"	160#	ST	15000		sat		65/ 98/190566	2800 gals	10 tons	58-9'	
18x24"	S	69"	165#	ST	15806	16%	sat		65/ 98/190566	2800 gals	10 tons	56-8'	[267-268]

Unknown — Rebuilt by Chicago & Grand Trunk – Fort Gratiot — 1891 & 1892 — (2) Acquired by CNR 3-01-1923

	Serial	Shipped	New as	1888	Rebuilt	1898	1900	11-1904	1-1910	Disposition
			—	—		—	—	H2	H2	
267	??	-??	??	**C&GT 70**	1891	**C&GT 1130**	***GTW* 1130**	***GTW* 1130**	***GTW* 2294**	Sc 7-14-26 UB
268	??	-??	??	**C&GT 98**	1892 4-4-0	**C&GT 1199**	***GTW* 1199**	***GTW* 1199**	***GTW* 2295**	Sc 10-24-27 UB

The complete history of the order for **267** and **268** is under GTW A-15-c 159-160 (page A-22). **Chicago & Grand Trunk Railroad 98**, built as a Vauclain compound, was likely built simple by C&GT in 1892.

CNR 269 — 4-4-0 EIGHT-WHEEL TYPE — B-13-a

Cylinder	Gear	Driv.	Pressure	Boiler	T.E.	Haulage	Steam	Stkr.	Drivers/Eng./Total	Water	Coal	Length	Notes
Specifications							Appliances		Weights	Fuel Capacity		Length	Notes
17x24"	S	73½"	#		00		sat		/ / 000	gals	tons	- '	[orig]
18x24"	S	69"	140#	ST	13000		sat		55/ 87/ 000	gals	tons	54-6'	

Canadian Locomotive & Engine Company — 1883 — (C-7) — (1) Acquired by CNR 3-01-1923

	Serial	Shipped	Ordered as	New as	1898	11-1904	1-1910	Disposition
			—	—	—	H9	H9	
(269)	231	2- -83	**GWR 219**	**GTR 758**	**GTR 521**	**GTR 402**	**GTR 2194**	Sc 10-14-29 MP
—	232	2- -83	GWR 221	GTR 759	GTR 522	GTR 403		Sc 9- -08

Yes, the photographs are of the same locomotive, and are arranged in chronological order. The top image of **GTR 2194** was made at Stratford in 1923, three years before it was authorized for scrapping. Dismantling was stayed, however, because of historical celebrations and the age of the 4-4-0. [AL PATERSON COLLECTION]

With its second style of stack and post 1918 identification, 269 as **GTR 2194** posed for another photographer at Toronto's first Spadina yard, likely in the spring of 1927. Besides the obvious alterations made to the stack, headlight and tender bunker for "cordwood", one major appliance was removed. The turbo-generator (for electric lighting) never appeared in any post-1926 photographs of 269. [H.L. GOLDSMITH/GEORGE CARPENTER COLLECTION]

CNR 269 as T&NR 269 in its second set of commemorative lettering and numbering was at Barrie (Allandale) in July 1926, on its way to the Huntsville "Old Home Week" celebrations. [CNR PHOTO 6245 DETAIL/ W.D. (BILL) THOMSON COLLECTION]

Four months previously, 269 as **GTR 2194** posed for the company photographer with its three-car train during March 1926, on its way from Pointe St. Charles to Toronto. Within a short time Stratford had replaced the diamond stack with a balloon type to represent an even earlier historical period. [CNR PHOTO 3872/H.L. GOLDSMITH/GEORGE CARPENTER COLLECTION]

CNR 269 was one of two locomotives ordered by the **Great Western Railway of Canada** as odd-numbered passenger locomotives numbers 219 and 221, but may have been delivered as **Grand Trunk Railway of Canada** 758-759 four months after the August 12th 1882 amalgamation of the two companies.

CNR 269 was the oldest Kingston-built locomotive acquired by CNR between 1919 and 1923, and as such was used for historical events and display between 1926 and 1927. The sequence of events is believed to be as follows:

(a) **GTR 2194** was approved for scrapping on March 19th 1926, but at the request from Huntsville representatives was resurrected from the Stratford scrap line and made operational including a diamond stack as GTR 2194. It became part of a train consisting of three cars from Pointe St. Charles – a baggage (CNR 8078), a combine (CNR 7414) and a coach (CNR 3177). The lettering and numbering on the locomotive were in the GTR style of 1910, namely "Grand Trunk" on the cab, and "2194" on the tender. The three cars were lettered "Grand Trunk Railway", although they retained their CNR road numbers. The train operated under its own power to Toronto during March of 1926.

(b) **T&NR 269**, relettered and renumbered from GTR 2194, was altered by the installation of a balloon stack at the Toronto shops, sometime in May and June of 1926. The cars were also relettered "Toronto and Nipissing Rly". The baggage car retained its CNR number, but panelling was applied to the combine and coach, and they appeared to have been renumbered. The train operated to Huntsville for the town's "Old Home Week", held between July 31st and August 6th 1926, which coincided with the 40th anniversary of

(text continues on next page)

CNR 269 as **GTR 269** *TREVITHICK* was at Toronto in September 1927 ready for a pose with the new U-2-a 4-8-4 6100 before the latter left for the Baltimore exhibition. [Al Paterson collection]

the opening of the rail line between Gravenhurst and North Bay.

(c) **GTR 2194** was probably re-converted during late 1926 or early 1927 upon its return to Stratford from the Huntsville celebration. It retained the balloon stack but reverted back to the GTR 1910 style of markings as in the March 1926 restoration.

(d) **GTR 269** was again changed to pose beside the first CNR 4-8-4, 6100, at the time the latter was being readied at Toronto to go to the B&O Railroad Centenary Exhibition which was held during August and September 1927. It was lettered "*TREVITHICK*" on the cab and "G.T.R. No. 269" in a nineteenth century style of lettering on the tender. The locomotive itself, including the balloon stack, remained unaltered.

To compare the 1926-1927 restoration, a photograph of the original **GTR *TREVITHICK*** is shown below.
The *TREVITHICK* of May 1859, named after the first locomotive superintendent, was GTR 209. It was the first of 602 steamers to be built at the railway's Pointe St. Charles shops.
[CNR PHOTO/H.L. GOLDSMITH/GEORGE CARPENTER COLLECTION]

Presumably the locomotive was held for possible use after 1927, but never did return to regular service. It was approved for scrapping on July 17th 1929 and scrapped at Stratford October 14th 1929.

CNR 270-276 — 4-4-0 EIGHT-WHEEL TYPE — B-14-a

Cylinder	Gear	Driv.	Pressure	Boiler	T.E.	Haulage	Steam	Stkr.	Drivers/Eng./Total	Water	Coal	Length	Notes
18x24"	S	69"	150#	ST	14000	14%	sat		63/102/ 000	gals	tons	57-6'	

Grand Trunk Railway – Pointe St. Charles 1882-1883 $11,200 — (7) Acquired by CNR 3-01-1923

	Serial	Shipped	New as	1898	11-1904	1-1910	Leased **TIR**	Disposition	To
			—	—	H4	H4	B-14-a		
270	1110	10- -82	**GTR 235***	**GTR 540**	**GTR 415**	**GTR 2197**		Sc 9- -25 HQ	
271	1111	10- -82	**GTR 236**	**GTR 541**	**GTR 416**	**GTR 2198**	12-27 to 8-32	Sc 8-15-32 HQ	
272	1112	11- -82	**GTR 237**	**GTR 542**	**GTR 417**	**GTR 2199**		Sc 6-22-25 HQ	
—	1113	11- -82	GTR 238	GTR 564	GTR 436	GTR 2226			**CNR 298**
273	1114	11- -82	**GTR 239**	**GTR 543**	**GTR 418**	**GTR 2200**		Sc 6-04-26 LM	
274	1115	12- -82	**GTR 240**	**GTR 544**	**GTR 419**	**GTR 2201**		Sc 5-12-26 LM	
275	1116	12- -82	**GTR 241**	**GTR 545**	**GTR 420**	**GTR 2202**		Sc 4-27-26 HQ	
276	1117	12- -82	**GTR 242**	**GTR 546**	**GTR 421**	**GTR 2203**		Sc 9- -25 HQ	
—	1118	1- -83	GTR 243	GTR 547	GTR 422	GTR 2211			**CNR 284**
—	1119	2- -83	GTR 244*	GTR 548	GTR 423	GTR 2212			**CNR 285**

CNR 270-276 were seven of ten 4-4-0s built by the **Grand Trunk Railway of Canada. CNR 271** was leased to the **Thousand Islands Railway** between 1927 and 1932 replacing CNR 242 on the line.

Following a trend in the 1880s to photograph locomotives in primer to highlight the details, **GTR 235** (270) was at Pointe St. Charles in October 1882.
[GTR PHOTO/H.L. GOLDSMITH & LEN HILLYARD/ GEORGE CARPENTER COLLECTION]
The engineer of much altered **GTR 2199** (272) awaiting signals in an unidentified location on Toronto's Esplanade about 1917.
[AL PATERSON COLLECTION]

CNR 274 was set out for retirement at London in 1925. Both engines and tenders had undergone alterations throughout their service careers. The original trucks and wheels under 235's tender had long been replaced before the tender was lowered on the frame in 1912. By 1925 Symington trucks had replaced the archbars under 2199's tender.
[*CNR LOCOMOTIVE DATA CARD*]

CNR 277-283 — 4-4-0 EIGHT-WHEEL TYPE — B-14-a

Cylinder	Gear	Driv.	Pressure	Boiler	T.E.	Haulage	Steam	Stkr.	Drivers/Eng./Total	Water	Coal	Length	Notes
Specifications							Appliances		Weights	Fuel Capacity		Length	Notes
18x24"	S	60"	150#		14000		sat		/102/ 000	gals	tons	- '	[orig GTR 94-101]
18x24"	S	69"	150#	ST	14000	14%	sat		63/102/ 000	gals	tons	*a:* 57-6' *b:* 58-8'	
18x24"	S	69"	165#	ST	16000	16%	sat		63/102/ 000	gals	tons	*c:* 57-6' *d:* 58-8'	

Grand Trunk Railway – Pointe St. Charles 1883 $9614 (277-281); $10,094 (282-283) (7) Acquired by CNR 3-01-1923

	Serial	Shipped	New as	1898	11-1904	11-1904	1-1910	1-1910	*OL*	Disposition	To
			—	—	H4	H8	H4	H8			
—	1130	8- -83	GTR 94	GTR 561		GTR 433		GTR 2223			**CNR 295**
277	1131	8- -83	**GTR 95**	**GTR 533**	**GTR 408**		**GTR 2204**		*b*	Sc 9- -23 MP	
278	1132	9- -83	**GTR 96**	**GTR 534**	**GTR 409**		**GTR 2205**		*c*	Sc 2-24-25 LM	
279	1133	9- -83	**GTR 97**	**GTR 535**	**GTR 410**		**GTR 2206**		*d*	Sc 2-18-25 LM	
—	1134	9- -83	GTR 98	GTR 562		GTR 434		GTR 2224			**CNR 296**
280/1	1135	10- -83	**GTR 99**	**GTR 536**	**GTR 411**		**GTR 2207**		*d*	Sc 6-09-27 LM	
—	1136	10- -83	GTR 100	GTR 563		GTR 435		GTR 2225			**CNR 297**
281	1137	10- -83	**GTR 101**	**GTR 537**	**GTR 412**		**GTR 2208**		*d*	Sc 9- -23 MP	
282	1138	11- -83	**GTR 233**	**GTR 538**	**GTR 413**		**GTR 2209**		*a*	Sc 12-28-27 LM	
283	1139	12- -83	**GTR 234**	**GTR 539**	**GTR 414**		**GTR 2210**		*b*	Sc 12-27-24 HQ	

CNR 277-283 were seven of ten 4-4-0s built by the **Grand Trunk Railway of Canada.** GTR 94-101 were converted from 60- to 69-inch drivers between 1887 and 1890. CNR 282 was slated for retirement in 1925, but was returned to service the same year.

CNR 280 (second)

See CNR Newfoundland Division list

CNR 284-285 — 4-4-0 EIGHT-WHEEL TYPE — B-14-a

Cylinder	Gear	Driv.	Pressure	Boiler	T.E.	Haulage	Steam	Stkr.	Drivers/Eng./Total	Water	Coal	Length	Notes
Specifications							Appliances		Weights	Fuel Capacity		Length	Notes
18x24"	S	69"	150#	ST	14000	14%	sat		63/102/ 000	4500 gals	tons	*a:* 57-6' *b:* 58-8'	[by 1913]

Grand Trunk Railway – Pointe St. Charles 1883 $11,200 (2) Acquired by CNR 3-01-1923

	Serial	Shipped	New as	1898	11-1904	1-1910	*OL*	Disposition	To
			—	—	H4	H4			
284	1118	1- -83	**GTR 243**	**GTR 547**	**GTR 422**	**GTR 2211**	*b*	Sc 7-08-25	
285	1119	2- -83	**GTR 244**	**GTR 548**	**GTR 423**	**GTR 2212**	*a*	Sc 1- -27	**LDL**

The complete history of the order for **284-285** is under CNR 270-276. **CNR 285** was sold for $2500 to **Lucien Dussault** from La Sarre, Quebec on the former NTR. It was moved to its new owner in Giffard, Quebec, on the QRL&P via Quebec City. Its final disposition after the sale is unknown.

CNR 286-290 — 4-4-0 EIGHT-WHEEL TYPE — B-15-a

Cylinder	Gear	Driv.	Pressure	Boiler	T.E.	Haulage	Steam	Stkr.	Drivers/Eng./Total	Water	Coal	Length	Notes
Specifications							Appliances		Weights	Fuel Capacity		Length	Notes
18x24"	S	74⅝"	180#	ST	15943		sat		68/109/225624	3750 gals	10 tons	58-8'	[2214-2216/286-288]
18x24"	S	69"	180#	ST	17000	17%	sat		68/109/225624	3750 gals	10 tons	57-2'	[2217-2218/290]
18x24"	S	69"	180#	ST	17242	17%	sat		68/109/225624	3750 gals	10 tons	57-2'	[289]

Grand Trunk Railway – Pointe St. Charles 1893 $10,000 (5) Acquired by CNR 3-01-1923

	Serial	Shipped	New as	1898	11-1904	1-1910	75>69"	Superheated	Disposition
			—	—	H5	H5		H11 EsC	
286	1274	6- -93	**GTR 82**	**GTR 553***	**GTR 424**	**GTR 2214**			Sc 12-12-25 HQ
287	1275	6- -93	**GTR 83**	**GTR 554**	**GTR 425**	**GTR 2215**			Sc 12-31-24 HQ
288	1276	6- -93	**GTR 84**	**GTR 555**	**GTR 426**	**GTR 2216**	11-17 GP		Sc 4-22-27 LM
289	1277	6- -93	**GTR 85**	**GTR 556**	**GTR 427**	**GTR 2217**	-nd	1-23 HQ	Sc 7-15-32 JD
290	1278	6- -93	**GTR 86***	**GTR 557**	**GTR 428**	**GTR 2218**	5-15 HQ		Sc 7-27-26 LM

CNR 286-290 were built with 61½-inch drivers, in 1893, three were changed to 74⅝ inches. Later **288-290** were fitted with 69-inch drivers. A Universal steam chest replaced the slide valves when **GTR 2217** was superheated.

GTR 86 (290) was posed after being converted to 74½-inch drivers in 1893 at Pointe St. Charles shops.
[CNR PHOTO 17093/FRITZ LEHMANN COLLECTION]

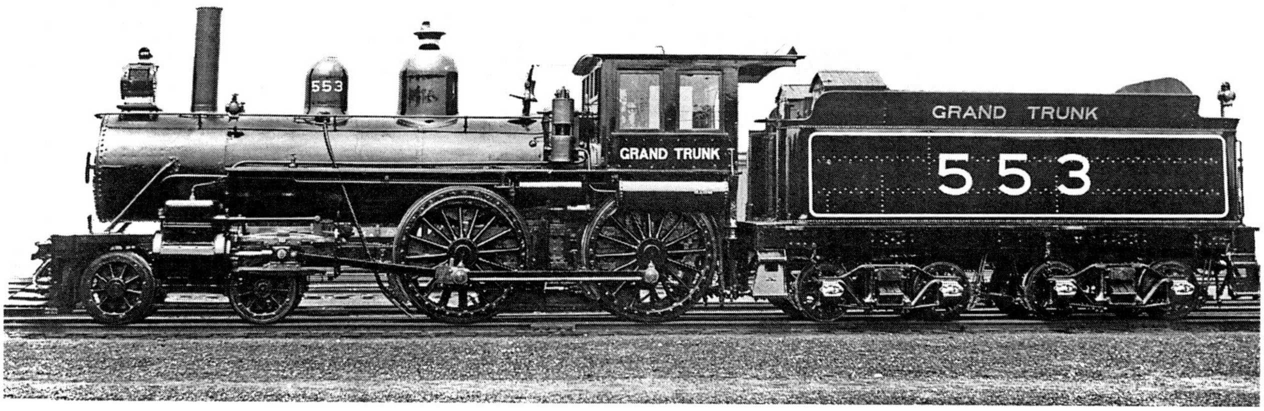

Although similarly converted, GTR 553 (286) at Pointe St. Charles in 1898 had headlight, cab, and tender truck upgrades.
[GTR PHOTO/H.L. GOLDSMITH/GEORGE CARPENTER COLLECTION]

GTR 427 (289), at an unidentified location in Montreal in June 1907, was one of two modified with 69-inch drivers.
[C.A. BUTCHER/WES DENGATE COLLECTION]

Saturated with inside steam pipes **GTR 2215** (287), likely at Pointe St. Charles soon after its renumbering in 1910, still relied on kerosene for lighting and had yet to be modified to improve crew safety with the addition of tender handrails and footholds. [GTR PHOTO/H.L. GOLDSMITH/GEORGE CARPENTER COLLECTION]

A factor in keeping **289** in service five years after the retirement of others in the class was because it was the only one in the group to be superheated. It takes a photograph such as the one of 289 and 4-8-2 6029, likely in Stratford during July 1924, to add a sense of scale to the actual size of the 4-4-0s. Both steamers exhibited the two styles of front ends prevalent on the National until the end of the 1920s. [CNR PHOTO/H.L. GOLDSMITH/GEORGE CARPENTER COLLECTION]

CNR 291-294 — 4-4-0 EIGHT-WHEEL TYPE — B-15-b

Specifications							Appliances		Weights	Fuel Capacity		Length	Notes
Cylinder	Gear	Driv.	Pressure	Boiler	T.E.	Haulage	Steam	Stkr.	Drivers/Eng./Total	Water	Coal		
18x24"	S	74⅝"	180#		16000		sat		/110/ 000	gals	tons	- '	[orig]
18x24"	S	74⅝"	185#	BEL	16000	16%	sat		68/109/ 000	4500 gals	tons	58-8'	[2221/293]
18x24"	S	69"	185#	BEL	18000	18%	sat		68/109/ 000	4500 gals	tons	58-8'	[2219-2220,2222/291-292,294]
18x24"	S	69"	180#	BEL	16000	16%	sat		68/109/ 000	4500 gals	tons	58-8'	[292]

Grand Trunk Railway – Pointe St. Charles 1890 $10,000 — (4) Acquired by CNR 3-01-1923

	Serial	Shipped	New as	BEL	1898	BEL	11-1904	1-1910	Disposition	To
			—		—		H8	H8		
292	1209	11- -90	**GTR 731**		**GTR 550**	1904?	**GTR 430**	**GTR 2220**	Sc 2-05-25 LM	
293	1210	11- -90	**GTR 732**		**GTR 551**	1904	**GTR 431**	**GTR 2221**	Sc 5-19-26 LM	
294	1211	11- -90	**GTR 733**		**GTR 552**	1904	**GTR 432**	**GTR 2222**	Sc 5-13-29 LM	
—	1212	11- -90	GTR 695	1897?	GTR 565		GTR 437	GTR 2227		**CNR 299**
291	1213	11- -90	**GTR 696**		**GTR 549**	1904	**GTR 429**	**GTR 2219**	Sc 12-28-27 LM	
—	1214	12- -90	GTR 697	1897	GTR 566		GTR 438	GTR 2228		**CNR 300**
—	1215	12- -90	GTR 698		GTR 567	1904	GTR 439	GTR 2229	Sc 4- -11	
—	1216	12- -90	GTR 699		GTR 568	1904	GTR 440	GTR 2230		**CNR 301**
—	1217	12- -90	GTR 700	1897	GTR 569		GTR 441	GTR 2231		**CNR 302**
—	1218	12- -90	GTR 701	1897	GTR 570		GTR 442	GTR 2232		**CNR 303**

CNR 291-294 were from ten locomotives built by the **Grand Trunk Railway of Canada** with 74⅝-inch drivers. The four were rebuilt with new Belpaire fireboxes, although no conversion date for GTR 430 was recorded.

CNR 299-303 were also built with 74½-inch drivers. GTR 437-442 were all rebuilt with Belpaire fireboxes except that no date was recorded for either GTR 437 or 440.

Numerous changes in specifications took place throughout the lives of the future B-15-b class. One of ten built in 1882-1883, **GTR 2223** (295), eventually acquired larger drivers, a Belpaire firebox and higher boiler pressure. At Stratford's "Big Shop" about 1923 the 69-inch-driver 4-4-0 was also equipped with a turbo-generator. **CNR 293**, at the same location about 1925, was from a lot of ten built in 1890. It was one of four which retained its original driver diameter of 74½-inches, but with absence of a headlight and dynamo, appeared to be undergoing conversion to electricity. [BOTH: AL PATERSON COLLECTION]

CNR 295-298 — 4-4-0 EIGHT-WHEEL TYPE — B-15-b

Specifications							Appliances		Weights	Fuel Capacity		Length	Notes
Cylinder	Gear	Driv.	Pressure	Boiler	T.E.	Haulage	Steam	Stkr.	Drivers/Eng./Total	Water	Coal		
18x24"	S	69"	180#	BEL	17000	17%	sat		67/107/ 000	4500 gals	tons	57-6'	[2223-2226/295-298]

Grand Trunk Railway – Pointe St. Charles			1882-1890	$9614			(4) Acquired by CNR 3-01-1923
	Serial	Shipped	New as	BEL	1898	11-1904	1-1910	Disposition
			—		—	H8	H8	
295	1130	8- -83	**GTR 94**	1897	**GTR 561**	**GTR 433**	**GTR 2223**	Sc 7-08-25 LM
296	1134	9- -83	**GTR 98**	1896	**GTR 562**	**GTR 434**	**GTR 2224**	Sc 10- -25 LM
297	1136	10- -83	**GTR 100**	1897	**GTR 563**	**GTR 435**	**GTR 2225**	Sc 10- -25 LM
298	1113	11- -82	**GTR 238**	1896	**GTR 564**	**GTR 436**	**GTR 2226**	Sc 10- -25 LM

CNR 295-297 had been built with 60-inch drivers by the **Grand Trunk Railway of Canada**, but were converted to 69-inch drivers between 1887-1890. See the complete order history under CNR 277-283 (page B-20).

298, built in a group of ten, originally had 69-inch drivers. See the complete note under CNR 270-276 (page B-18).

CNR 299-303 (first) 4-4-0 EIGHT-WHEEL TYPE B-15-c

Cylinder	Gear	Driv.	Pressure	Boiler	T.E.	Haulage	Steam	Stkr.	Drivers/Eng./Total	Water	Coal	Length	Notes
Specifications							Appliances		Weights	Fuel Capacity			
18x24"	S	74⅝"	180#	BEL	16000	16%	sat		70/110/ 000	4500 gals	tons	58-8'	[2228,2232/300,303]
18x24"	S	74⅝"	185#	BEL	16000	16%	sat		70/110/ 000	4500 gals	tons	58-8'	[2230/301]
18x24"	S	69"	180#	BEL	17000	17%	sat		70/110/ 000	4500 gals	tons	58-8'	[2227,2231/299,302]

Grand Trunk Railway – Pointe St. Charles 1890 $10,000 (5) Acquired by CNR 3-01-1923

	Serial	Shipped	New as	BEL	1898	11-1904	BEL	1-1910	Disposition
			—		—	H8		H8	
299	1212	11- -90	**GTR 695**	nd	**GTR 565**	**GTR 437**		**GTR 2227**	Sc 9- -25 LM
300/1	1214	12- -90	**GTR 697**	1897	**GTR 566**	**GTR 438**		**GTR 2228**	Sc 9- -25 LM
301/1	1216	12- -90	**GTR 699**		**GTR 568**	**GTR 440**	1904	**GTR 2230**	Sc 5-08-28 LM
302/1	1217	12- -90	**GTR 700**	1897	**GTR 569**	GTR 441		**GTR 2231**	Sc 1-22-25 LM
303/1	1218	12- -90	**GTR 701**	1897	**GTR 570**	**GTR 442**		**GTR 2232**	Sc 5-08-28 LM

CNR 299-303. See note under 291-294 (page B-22).

The 74½-inch drivers of 301, out-of-service in Turcot yard Montreal in April 1928, were twice as large as the young boy posing for his photograph. The real admirer was likely behind the camera. The 4-4-0, similar to others in the B-15 classes, had been rebuilt with a Belpaire firebox, acquired a dynamo, handrails and footholds, a lowered tender body, and a steel-plated cab. Dismantling of 301 was only weeks away. [H.K. VOLLRATH/WES DENGATE COLLECTION]

CNR 304-308 (first) 4-4-0 EIGHT-WHEEL TYPE B-16-a

Cylinder	Gear	Driv.	Pressure	Boiler	T.E.	Haulage	Steam	Stkr.	Drivers/Eng./Total	Water	Coal	Length	Notes
Specifications							Appliances		Weights	Fuel Capacity			
18x24"	S	69"	180#	WT	17000	17%	sat		64/100/ 000	gals	tons	55-7'	

Baldwin Locomotive Works – Burnham, Williams & Company 1893-1895 $12,000 (5) Acquired by CNR 3-01-1923

	Serial	Shipped	New as	8-1899	1-1905	1-1910	Disposition
			—	F	H2	H2	
304/1	13700	8- -93	**OA&PS / CAR 20**	**CAR 621**	**GTR 1324**	**GTR 2233**	Sc 7-23-25 HQ
305/1	13699	8- -93	**OA&PS / CAR 21**	**CAR 622**	**GTR 1325**	**GTR 2234**	Sc 6-22-25 HQ
306/1	13991	4- -94	**CAR 22**	**CAR 623**	**GTR 1326**	**GTR 2235**	Sc 7-09-25 HQ
307/1	13992	4- -94	**CAR 23**	**CAR 624**	**GTR 1327**	**GTR 2236**	Sc 11-20-25 HQ
308/1	14296	3- -95	**V&PL / CAR 30**	**CAR 625**	**GTR 1328**	**GTR 2237**	Sc 7-02-25 HQ

CNR 304-308 came from three orders built for the **Ottawa, Arnprior & Parry Sound Railway** and the **Canada Atlantic Railway.** Numbers 20 and 21 (304 and 305) were shipped from BLW in August 1893 and received in September 1893. Number **30** (308), built in March 1895 and shipped in April, although built for the CAR, was initially assigned to the leased **Vermont & Province Line Railroad.** CAR 622 and 623 were known to have been used on the OA&PS after 1899, before becoming **Grand Trunk Railway of Canada** 4-4-0s.

CAR 21 (305), at Alexandria, Ontario on January 24th 1895, was from the first of three lots delivered from Baldwin between 1893 and 1895. Two distinctive pieces of equipment prevalent during the period which gave the CAR 4-4-0s character were the splash guards on all wheels and the cap on the stack. All five 4-4-0s eventually were taken into CNR stock.

Despite some upgrades, particularly to the tender and the lighting system, **GTR 2236** (307), in the shops line at Pointe St. Charles sometime after 1917, had few structural changes since its introduction two decades earlier. Gone, of course, was the vertical slatted pilot with its pin-and-link coupling, and the kerosene box headlight.
[BOTH: H.L. GOLDSMITH/GEORGE CARPENTER COLLECTION]

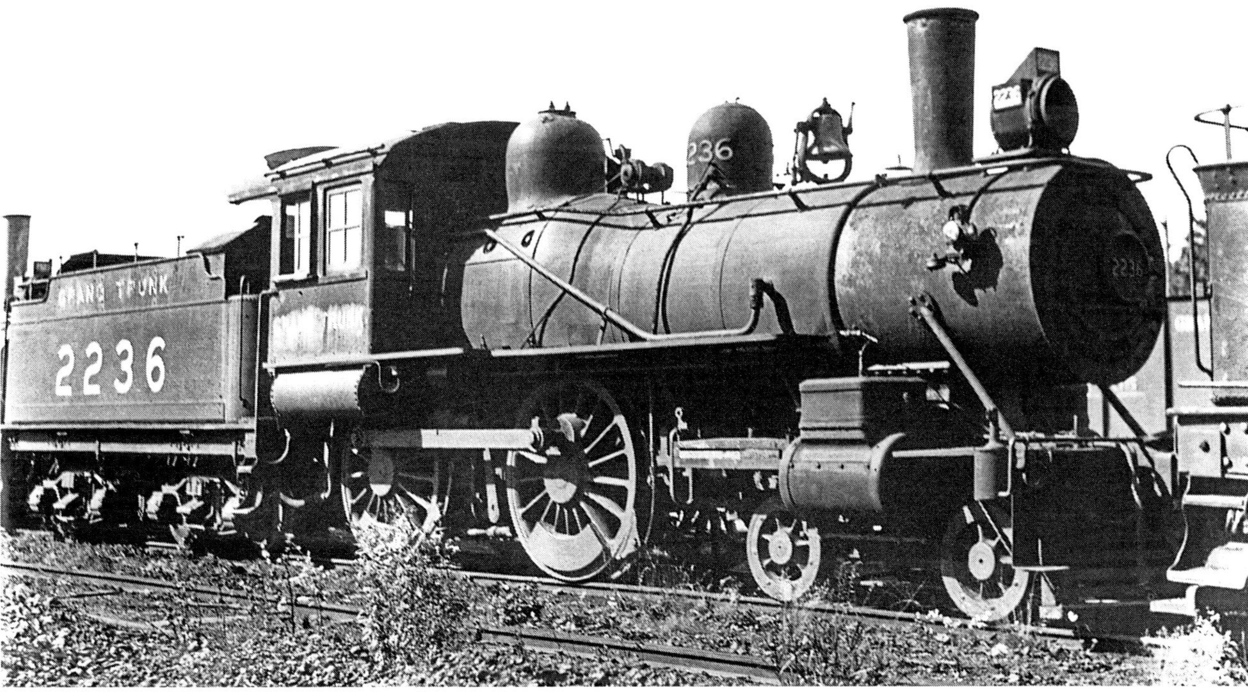

CNR 309-310 (first) — 4-4-0 EIGHT-WHEEL TYPE — B-16-b

Cylinder	Gear	Driv.	Pressure	Boiler	T.E.	Haulage	Steam	Stkr.	Drivers/Eng./Total	Water	Coal	Length	Notes
Specifications							Appliances		Weights	Fuel Capacity			
18x24"	S	69"	180#	WT	17000	17%	sat		68/106/ 000	gals	tons	55-0'	

Baldwin Locomotive Works - Burnham, Williams & Company 1896 $12,393 — (2) Acquired by CNR 3-01-1923

	Serial	Shipped	New as	8-1899	1-1905	1-1910	Disposition
			—	F	H7	H7	
309/1	15067	10- -96	**CAR 25**	**CAR 626**	**GTR 1329**	**GTR 2238**	Sc 7-23-25 HQ
310/1	15068	10- -96	**CAR 26**	**CAR 627**	**GTR 1330**	**GTR 2239**	Sc 11-20-25 HQ

CNR 309 and 310 were built for the **Canada Atlantic Railway** before being taken into the **Grand Trunk Railway of Canada** stock.

CNR 310, near the end of its career at Pointe St. Charles in 1928, represented the final phase in appearance of the former CAR 4-4-0s. Its own appearance had evolved from one very similar to that of CAR 21 (page B-25). The standard front-end treatment of the 1920s, with the centred headlight, triangular road number lamp and horizontally slatted pilot, accentuated the length of the extended smokebox. Other improvements included the addition of a dynamo, steel plating on the cab, and a flush steel letterboard on the tender. With the paint bleed on the side of the tender, the 4-4-0's heritage would never be in doubt. [*CNR LOCOMOTIVE DATA CARD*]

CNR 311 (first) — 4-4-0 EIGHT-WHEEL TYPE — B-17-a

Cylinder	Gear	Driv.	Pressure	Boiler	T.E.	Haulage	Steam	Stkr.	Drivers/Eng./Total	Water	Coal	Length	Notes
Specifications							Appliances		Weights	Fuel Capacity			
18x24"	S	67"	#		18000		sat		/109/209000	gals	tons	- '	[orig]
18x24"	S	69"	180#	WT	17242	17%	sat		69/109/201000	4000 gals	8½ tons	58-8'	

Schenectady Locomotive Works 1896 $12,500 — (1) Acquired by CNR 3-01-1923

	Serial	Shipped	New as	1897	1898	11-1904	1-1910	Disposition
			—	—	G	H6	H6	
311/1	4437	2- -96	**SL&A 1 BEAUHARNOIS**	**CAR 24**	**CAR 628**	**GTR 1331**	**GTR 2240**	Sc 8- -25 HQ

CNR 311 was built for the **St. Lawrence & Adirondack Railroad** before its acquisition by the **Canada Atlantic Railway** and the **Grand Trunk Railway of Canada.** SL&A 1 may have been named *BEAUHARNOIS.*

CNR 312-313 (first) — 4-4-0 EIGHT-WHEEL TYPE — B-18-a

Cylinder	Gear	Driv.	Pressure	Boiler	T.E.	Haulage	Steam	Stkr.	Drivers/Eng./Total	Water	Coal	Length	Notes
Specifications							Appliances		Weights	Fuel Capacity			
18x24"	S	78"	#		00		sat		/ / 000	gals	tons	- '	[orig]
18x26"	S	74⅝"	150#	ST	14393	14%	sat		64/107/223300	3750 gals	10 tons	56-10'	[2232-2233/312]
18x26"	S	69"	150#	ST	15566	16%	sat		64/107/223300	3750 gals	10 tons	57-6'	[313]

Grand Trunk Railway – Pointe St. Charles 1881 $10,000 — (2) Acquired by CNR 3-01-1923

	Serial	Shipped	New as	1898	10-1899	11-1904	1-1910	74>69"	Disposition
			—	—	—	H	H		
312/1	1065	9- -81	**GTR 92**	**GTR 575**	**GTR 594**	**GTR 461**	**GTR 2332**		Sc 8-01-28 LM
313/1	1066	11- -81	**GTR 93***	**GTR 576**	**GTR 595**	**GTR 462**	**GTR 2333**	8-18 HQ	Sc 7-03-28 LM

CNR 312 and 313 were built by the **Grand Trunk Railway of Canada.**

Two early views of CNR 313 provide further evidence as to how much change was possible during the life of a 4-4-0 which was built in the nineteenth century and remained in service into the twentieth century. **GTR 93**, especially primered for the photographer, emerged from the company shops at Pointe St. Charles in 1881 with 78-inch drivers. [TANDY PHOTO/CNR PHOTO 17189/FRITZ LEHMANN COLLECTION]

Almost three decades later, a much-altered **GTR 462** was thought to be at the Komoka, Ontario gravel pit about 1906. Extending the wagon top boiler resulted in a redesigned and enlarged steam chest, as well as a change in the location of the headlight mounting. Although the colour of GTR 93 may only be guessed at, the shade of utilitarian black of the 462 would be a given. [DON McQUEEN COLLECTION]

CNR 314-315 (first) 4-4-0 EIGHT-WHEEL TYPE B-26-a

Cylinder	Gear	Driv.	Pressure	Boiler	T.E.	Haulage	Steam	Stkr.	Drivers/Eng./Total	Water	Coal	Length	Notes
Specifications							Appliances		Weights	Fuel Capacity			
18x24"	S	63"	200#		19000		sat		74/122/249660	5000 gals	10 tons	58-9'	[orig]
18x24"	S	69"	200#	EWT	19400	19%	sat		74/122/249660	5000 gals	10 tons	60-0½'	[1898-1926]

Canadian Locomotive & Engine Company 1886 (C-19) $10,000 — (2) Acquired by CNR 3-01-1923

	Serial	Shipped	New as	1888	nB	1898	10-1899	11-1904	Rebuilt	1-1910	Disposition
			—	—		—	—	H1		H1	
314/1	312	11?- -86	**N&NW 83**	**GTR 686**	1898	**GTR 527**	**GTR 571**	**GTR 443**	5-06	**GTR 1909**	Sc 12-05-25 LM
315/1	313	12-28-86	**N&NW 84**	**GTR 687**	1898	**GTR 528**	**GTR 572**	**GTR 444**	11-08	**GTR 1910**	Sc 4-30-26 LM

CNR **314** and **315** were two of six delivered to the **Northern & North Western Railway**. In 1888 all were renumbered into the **Grand Trunk Railway of Canada** roster. See the entry under A-12-a 130 and 131 for the complete history of the order (page A-13). In 1898 GTR 686 and 687 were rebuilt with new boilers and as a result assigned the first two numbers in CNR's large B-26-a class.

Although built with 63-inch drivers, the change of drivers in 1898 to 69 inches on **GTR 1910** (315), shown at Palmerston on May 30th 1923, resulted in the locomotive's placement into the large B-26-a class. Although it, and **314**, shown at the Stratford "Big Shop" about 1925, remained saturated machines with inside steam pipes, they set a specification standard for those built for the GTP more than twenty years later. [BOTH: AL PATERSON COLLECTION]

CNR 316-324 (first) — 4-4-0 EIGHT-WHEEL TYPE — B-26-a

Cylinder	Gear	Driv.	Pressure	Boiler	T.E.	Haulage	Steam	Stkr.	Weights Drivers/Eng./Total	Water	Coal	Length	Notes
		Specifications					Appliances			Fuel Capacity			
18x24"	S	63"	200#	EWT	19000		sat		74/121/ 000	gals	tons	58-9'	[orig]
18x24"	S	69"	200#	EWT	19200		sat		74/122/264900	5000 gals	10 tons	60-5'	[GTP 50]
18x24"	S	69"	200#	EWT	19200	19%	sat		74/128/249660	5000 gals	10 tons	60-0½'	[CNR]
18x24"	S	75"	200#	EWT	17714	18%	sat		74/128/249660	5000 gals	10 tons	60-0½'	[1917/321]
18x24"	S	69"	200#	EWT	19200	19%	sat		74/122/264900	5000 gals	10 tons	59-7½'	[324]

Grand Trunk Railway – Pointe St. Charles 1899 $9000 — (9) Acquired by CNR 3-01-1923

	Serial	Shipped	New as	1904	9-1909	1-1910	by 1913	Disposition
			—	H1	—	H1	H1	
316/1	1301	-99	**GTR 573**	**GTR 445**		**GTR 1911**		Sc 10-03-27 LM
317/1	1302	-99	**GTR 574**	**GTR 446**		**GTR 1912**		Sc 11-26-25 HQ
—	1303	-99	GTR 575	GTR 447		GTW 1913		Sc 12- -12
318/1	1304	-99	**GTR 576**	**GTR 448**		**GTR 1914**		Sc 4-27-27 C
319/1	1305	-99	**GTR 577**	**GTR 449**		**GTR 1915**		Sc 7-07-27 LM
320/1	1306	-99	**GTR 578**	**GTR 450**		**GTR 1916**		Sc 9-10-27 LM
321/1	1307	-99	**GTR 579**	**GTR 451**		**GTR 1917**		Sc 4-27-27 C
322/1	1308	-99	**GTR 580**	**GTR 452**		**GTR 1918**		Sc 6-16-27 C
323/1	1309	-99	**GTR 581**	**GTR 453**		**GTR 1919**		Sc 4-27-27 C
324/1	1310	-99	**GTR 582**	**GTR 454**	**GTP 300**		**GTP 50**	Sc 11-01-38 AK

B-26-a

CNR 316-324 were built for the **Grand Trunk Railway of Canada.** GTR 454 (324) was transferred to the **Grand Trunk Pacific Railway** and renumbered from GTP 300 to GTP 50 sometime between September 1909 and 1913.

GTR 1911 (316), at the Lehigh Valley station in Buffalo, New York during May 1917, was representative of the second lot built which would become part of the B-26-a class. The change to 69-inch drivers inaugurated in 1898 (above) apparently found favour with the rolling stock department, for all ten in this lot which followed a year later were built with the same dimensions. The 1911, with its characteristic safety valve housing mounted above the firebox had, by the time the photograph was taken, acquired a steel cab and a centred headlight, although the latter was still burning kerosene.
[KARL E. SCHLACHTER PHOTO/GEORGE CARPENTER COLLECTION]

CNR 325-399 — 4-4-0 EIGHT-WHEEL TYPE — B-26-a

CNR 325-399 were all built as passenger locomotives for the **Grand Trunk Pacific Railway**. The first fifty (**CNR 325-374**) were part of an order placed by the **Grand Trunk Railway of Canada** for one hundred locomotives in December 1907. The GTR component of the order included twenty 2-8-0s (CNR 2627-2646), ten 4-6-0s (CNR 1619-1628), ten 2-6-0s (CNR 698-707), and ten 0-6-0s (CNR 7155-7157 and 7202-7208).

The ten 4-4-0s sold to the **Canadian Northern Railway** did not receive their CNR-assigned numbers until 1920. Twelve GTP 4-4-0s were converted to oil at Transcona (PU) during 1915 and 1916, and eight others had Hungerford & Cameron (H-C) superheater units applied with Economy (Universal) steam chests (EsC) between 1920 and 1923. (See Appendices BO and BC).

The saturated 4-4-0s were the first to be removed from the CNR roster.

As B-26-a engines were withdrawn, many of their tenders were applied to a variety of other types or were adapted for OCS use. The transfers to other locomotives are outlined in Appendix DD. Before being renumbered to **334**, its tender, as GTP 60, may have been assigned OCS auxiliary tender number **CN 51571** (first) in 1928, but whether it was put into service is not known, for within a year the number was transferred to the tender of **375**. **CN 51571** (second), taken from **375** in 1929, was used as an Atlantic Region auxiliary tender until scrapped in August 1958. It is assumed both 334 and 375 received tenders from other members of the class which had been retired.

CNR 325-354 (first) — 4-4-0 EIGHT-WHEEL TYPE — B-26-a

Specifications							Appliances		Weights	Fuel Capacity		Length	Notes
Cylinder	Gear	Driv.	Pressure	Boiler	T.E.	Haulage	Steam	Stkr.	Drivers/Eng./Total	Water	Coal		
18x24"	S	69"	200#	EWT	19200		sat		74/122/264900	5000 gals	10 tons	60-5'	[GTP]
18x24"	S	69"	180#	EWT	17000		sat		74/122/264900	5830 gals	10 tons	59-7½'	[by 1913 to 1920]
18x24"	S	69"	200#	EWT	19200	19%	sat		74/122/264900	5830 gals	3000 gals	59-7½'	[oil]
18x24"	S	69"	200#	EWT	19200	19%	H-C		75/125/267800	5830 gals	10 tons	59-7½'	
18x24"	S	63"	200#	EWT	20980	21%	sat		74/122/264900	5830 gals	3000 gals	59-7½'	[337 by 1920]

Montreal Locomotive Works - ALCO 1908 (Q-81) $15,000
(30) Acquired by CNR 3-01-1919 (CaNoR); or (GTP) operated and managed by CNR 7-12-1920; acquired 1-31-1923

	Serial	Shipped	New as	10-1918	To oil	Superheated	Leased to	Mods	Tender to	Disposition	To
			H1	B-7-A		EsC					
325/1	44822	4- -08	**GTP 51**	**CaNoR 70**						Sc 10-02-35 C	
326/1	44823	4- -08	**GTP 52**	**CaNoR 71**						Sc 12-09-35 C	
327/1	44824	4- -08	**GTP 53**							So 12- -27 A	**MSCo**
328/1	44825	4- -08	**GTP 54**							Sc 5-28-26 PU	
329/1	44826	4- -08	**GTP 55**							Sc 6-10-26 W	
330	44827	4- -08	**GTP 56**							Sc 6-15-28 W	
331	44828	4- -08	**GTP 57**			3-22 PU		w		Sc 8-26-38 W	
332	44829	4- -08	**GTP 58**							Sc 7-25-27 W	
333	44830	4- -08	**GTP 59**							Sc 10-20-25 MV	
334	44831	4- -08	**GTP 60**				**BMPCo** 1926-27		**CN 51571**/1	So 3- -33 A	**MSCo**
335	44832	4- -08	**GTP 61**		2-15 PU					Sc 10-17-38 W	
336	44833	4- -08	**GTP 62***			12-20 PU		w		Sc 9-13-35 PU	
337	44834	4- -08	**GTP 63**		7-15 PU					Sc 10-29-28 W	
338	44835	4- -08	**GTP 64**	**CaNoR 72**						Sc 9- -25 MV	
339	44836	4- -08	**GTP 65**		2-15 PU					Sc 7-31-26 PU	
340	44837	4- -08	**GTP 66**			3-22 PU		w		Sc 10-26-35 W	
341	44838	4- -08	**GTP 67**				**MSCo** 1926-27			Sc 6-18-35 W	
342	44839	4- -08	**GTP 68**							Sc 5-31-27 W	
343	44840	4- -08	**GTP 69**							Sc 7-07-27 W	
344	44841	4- -08	**GTP 70**							Sc 11- -25 MV	
345	44842	4- -08	**GTP 71**		7-14 PU			w		Sc 12-17-35 W	
346	44843	4- -08	**GTP 72**							Sc 6-16-26 W	
347	44844	4- -08	**GTP 73**							Sc 10- -25 MV	
348	44845	5- -08	**GTP 74**			3-22 PU				Sc 5-30-31 W	
349	44846	5- -08	**GTP 75**						**CN 899**	Sc 7-20-27 RH	
350	44847	5- -08	**GTP 76**							Sc 7-27-27 W	
351	44848	5- -08	**GTP 77**			3-22 PU		w		Sc 4-30-37 W	
352	44849	5- -08	**GTP 78**	**CaNoR 73**				w		Sc 1-07-36 MQ	
353	44850	5- -08	**GTP 79**							Sc 6-16-27 W	
354	44851	5- -08	**GTP 80**	**CaNoR 74**						Sc 4-30-29 C	

Notes for **CNR 325-354** are under the general note for CNR B-26-a 325-399 (page B-30). **CNR 334** was leased to **Bowaters Mersey Paper** at Brooklyn, Nova Scotia between 1926 and 1927. **CNR 341** was leased to the **Malagash Salt Company** in Malagash, Nova Scotia, and was returned when **327** was purchased in December 1927. In turn 327 was replaced by **334** in 1933, and in 1935 it was replaced by **394**. All three were scrapped at Malagash by **Garsons**: **327** in 1933, **334** in 1936, and **394** in the year 1951.

To satisfy its need for a locomotive to power its light passenger trains, the GTP drew upon the specifications of the parent's H1 class 4-4-0s. **GTP 62** (336) at Montreal in April 1908 was in the first of three lots built for the western road's H1 class. The more compact safety valve housing (later modified) and a tender with a larger capacity than its GTR forerunners were notable design differences. [MLW PHOTO Q-81/H.L. GOLDSMITH/GEORGE CARPENTER COLLECTION]

B-26-a

CNR 331, at Port Mann on June 26th 1929, was not one of the four to be converted to oil during World War I, but was one of five superheated with Universal piston valves during the early 1920s. [AL PATERSON COLLECTION]

CNR 300-329 (second)

See CNR Newfoundland Division list (pages Nfld-5 to Nfld-16

CNR 355-374 — 4-4-0 EIGHT-WHEEL TYPE — B-26-a

Specifications							Appliances		Weights	Fuel Capacity		Length	Notes
Cylinder	Gear	Driv.	Pressure	Boiler	T.E.	Haulage	Steam	Stkr.	Drivers/Eng./Total	Water	Coal		
18x24"	S	69"	200#	EWT	19200		sat		74/122/264900	5000 gals	10 tons	60-5'	[GTP]
18x24"	S	69"	200#	EWT	19200	19%	sat		74/122/264900	5830 gals	3000 gals	59-7½'	[oil]

Canada Foundry Company Limited – Davenport Works 1908 $15,000
(20) Acquired by CNR 3-01-1919 (CaNoR); or (GTP) operated and managed by CNR 7-12-1920; acquired 1-31-1923

	Serial	Shipped	New as	10-1918	To oil	To coal	Oil Equipment	Mods	Disposition
			H1	B-7-A			to		
355	909	7- -08	**GTP 81**						Sc 5-28-26 W
356	910	7- -08	**GTP 82**						Sc 7-15-26 W
357	911	8- -08	**GTP 83**						Sc 5-28-26 W
358	912	8- -08	**GTP 84**	**CaNoR 75**					Sc 12-09-35 C
359	913	8- -08	**GTP 85**	**CaNoR 76**					Sc 9- -25 MV
360	914	8- -08	**GTP 86**		3-16 PU			w	Sc 9-29-38 W
361	915	8- -08	**GTP 87**		3-16 PU	7-37 PK	2091		Sc 11-23-38 W
362	916	8- -08	**GTP 88**						Sc 7-15-26 W
363	917	8- -08	**GTP 89**						Sc 7-31-26 W
364	918	8- -08	**GTP 90**		2-15 PU	8-37 PK	2124	w	Sc 11-04-38 W
365	919	9- -08	**GTP 91**						Sc 6-16-26 W
366	920	9- -08	**GTP 92**						Sc 10-20-25 MV
367	921	9- -08	**GTP 93**						Sc 11-30-32 A
368	922	10- -08	**GTP 94**						Sc 6-16-26 PU
369	923	10- -08	**GTP 95**		2-15 PU				Sc 7-31-26 W
370	924	10- -08	**GTP 96**						Sc 8-04-27 W
371	925	11- -08	**GTP 97**		3-15 PU				Sc 4-30-41 W
372	926	11- -08	**GTP 98**		3-15 PU			w	Sc 5-01-41 W
373	927	11- -08	**GTP 99**						Sc 6-24-27 SH
374	928	12- -08	**GTP 100**						Sc 10-03-27 LM

B-26-a

Sharing the GTP order for fifty 4-4-0s were twenty from Toronto's Canada Foundry. Two in the order were allocated to the power-short CaNoR during the last year of World War I. Although disappointingly cropped, this image of **CaNoR 76** (359) at Transcona just before 1920 was rare in that very few photographs were apparently taken of any of the transfers to CaNoR. The evidence identifying the CaNoR 4-4-0 from an identical GTP 76 (350) was the class and haulage rating on the cab. [*CNR LOCOMOTIVE DATA CARD*] See Vol. 1, p. 93 for a view of **CNR 371**, one of six in the lot converted to oil during World War I, still saturated but modified with outside steam pipes. [W. MONYPENY/GEORGE CARPENTER COLLECTION]

The notes for CNR 355-374 are under the general note for CNR B-26-a 325-399 (page B-30).

CNR 375-399 — 4-4-0 EIGHT-WHEEL TYPE — B-26-a

Specifications							Appliances		Weights	Fuel Capacity		Length	Notes
Cylinder	Gear	Driv.	Pressure	Boiler	T.E.	Haulage	Steam	Stkr.	Drivers/Eng./Total	Water	Coal		
18x24"	S	69"	200#	EWT	19200		sat		74/122/264900	5000 gals	10 tons	60-5'	[GTP]
18x24"	S	69"	200#	EWT	19200	19%	sat		74/122/264900	5830 gals	3000 gals	59-7½'	[oil]
18x24"	S	69"	200#	EWT	19200	19%	H-C		74/125/267800	5830 gals	10 tons	59-7½'	

Montreal Locomotive Works Limited - ALCO 1909 (Q-105) $14,000
(25) Acquired by CNR 3-01-1919 (CaNoR); or (GTP) operated and managed by CNR 7-12-1920; acquired 1-31-1923

	Serial	Shipped	New as	10-1918	To oil	Superheated	Mods	Tender to	c.1924	Disposition	To
			H1	B-7-A		EsC			Ls. to		
375	46078	7- -09	**GTP 101**					**CN 51571**/2	SER	Sc 11-30-32 A	
376	46079	7- -09	**GTP 102**							Sc 6-03-26 C	
377	46080	7- -09	**GTP 103**							Sc 7-15-26 W	
378	46081	7- -09	**GTP 104**							Sc 11-14-35 W	
379	46082	7- -09	**GTP 105**							Sc 6-06-27 W	
380	46083	7- -09	**GTP 106**	**CaNoR 77**			w			Sc 12-09-35 C	
381	46084	7- -09	**GTP 107**	**CaNoR 78**						Sc 10-31-35 C	
382	46085	7- -09	**GTP 108**							Sc 5-31-27 RH	
383	46086	7- -09	**GTP 109**							Sc 5-13-29 W	
384	46087	7- -09	**GTP 110***		3-15 PU					Sc 12-30-35 W	
385	46088	7- -09	**GTP 111**							Sc 7-14-27 W	
386	46089	7- -09	**GTP 112**				w			Sc 5-25-37 W	
387	46090	7- -09	**GTP 113**	**CaNoR 79**						Sc 4-05-37 W	
388	46091	7- -09	**GTP 114**			7-23 PU	w			Sc 5-01-37 W	
389	46092	7- -09	**GTP 115**			7-23 PU	w			Sc 7-12-37 W	
390	46093	7- -09	**GTP 116**		2-15 PU					Sc 8-11-26 W	
391	46094	7- -09	**GTP 117**							Sc 6-09-27 W	
392	46095	7- -09	**GTP 118**			4-23 PU	w			Sc 6-14-37 W	
393	46096	10- -09	**GTP 119**							Sc 11- -25 MV	
394	46097	10- -09	**GTP 120**						SER	So 12-23-35 AK	**MSCo**
395	46098	10- -09	**GTP 121**							Sc 6-17-27 W	
396	46099	10- -09	**GTP 122**							Sc 10- -25 MV	
397	46100	10- -09	**GTP 123**							Sc 10-31-33 AK	
398	46101	10- -09	**GTP 124**							Sc 5-08-28 LM	
399	46102	10- -09	**GTP 125**							Sc 5-31-28 C	

The final twenty-five in the GTP H1 class, built in 1909 by Montreal Locomotive Works were the last 4-4-0s to be produced in Canada, and pristine **GTP 125** (399), photographed seven months after its delivery on May 6th 1910, was the last in that order. It was on a train to Rivers, Manitoba, from the former Northern Pacific & Manitoba station on Water Street, Winnipeg. The GTP shared the facilities with the CaNoR before Union Station was opened in 1911. [GTP PHOTO?/DON McQUEEN COLLECTION]

Notes for **CNR 375-399** are under the general note for CNR B-26-a 325-399 (page B-30). The twenty-five were ordered from MLW in December 1908. About 1924, GTP 101 and 120 were transferred to operate the former **South Eastern Railway** and were immediately renumbered to CNR 375 and 394. See the note under CNR B-26-a 325-354 for sale details to the **Malagash Salt Company**. **CNR 397**, earmarked for removal in 1925, was returned to service later that year, and in 1931 was fitted with the steel cab from retired 2-8-0 1902. After its retirement in 1933, the boiler was installed for the Moncton reclamation yard plant in 1934.

CNR 392, believed to be heading train number 37 during 1926 on the approach to the Fraser River bridge in Surrey, west of Port Mann, was one of three to be superheated. The angle of view chosen by the photographer enhanced the outside steam pipe, piston valve chest, hanging running board steps, the blanked forward side windows and the built-up coal bunker.
[LAWRENCE A. STUCKEY PHOTO?/DON McQUEEN COLLECTION]

At Port Mann on June 23rd 1927, **392** had undergone some changes from when photographed a year earlier. Not only had one of the spoked engine truck wheels been changed out for a set of disks, but a hood had been installed above the headlight lens. What remained constant, however, was the CaNoR practice of using the upper case sub-letter in the class designation on the cab.
[SIRMAN AND AL PATERSON COLLECTIONS]

CONTENTS

VOLUME 2

VOLUME 3

VOLUME 4

VOLUME 5

VOLUME 6

VOLUME 7

VOLUME 8

NEWFOUNDLAND: 15-599

THIS SECTION

CNR 15-599 NEWFOUNDLAND DISTRICT

ALL TYPES

The day Newfoundland joined the Canadian Confederation, CNR inherited forty-six locomotives in four wheel arrangements from the railway it was about to operate. Six of these (five 4-6-0s and one 2-8-0) dated back to the **Reid-Newfoundland Company Limited** lease of the railway. The remaining forty (ten 4-6-2s and thirty Mikados) had all been built for the **Newfoundland Railway**. The last six, Mikado Types, arrived on the island in the same month as Confederation. The earlier history of Newfoundland locomotives can be found in Lavallée: *Narrow Gauge Railways of Canada* (both 1972 and 2005 editions).

CNR devised a three-digit road number series (to indicate the island's narrow gauge rail lines), assigning the first digit in the number to reflect the same digit used on mainland locomotives in the same wheel type: that is, "1" for the Ten Wheelers; "2" for the Consolidation; "3" for the Mikados, and "5" for the Pacifics. Two digits were used for the Ten Wheelers so as not to conflict with the three-digit 100-series already used for the Z class electrics. Although all Newfoundland District road numbers were second use on the CNR system, classification adhered to the 1919 master plan, with only the F-3-a class reused a second time.

All Newfoundland Railway locomotives taken into CNR stock were equipped with steam lines to provide heat to passenger equipment. They were also equipped with a flanger control device unique to the island. When needed, a flanger blade was mounted between the pilot and lead truck of the locomotive with the lifting apparatus permanently located on the pilot deck. The connecting rod to the fulcrum crank was linked to an air-activated cylinder which was located above the running board either on the right or left side of the locomotive. The location of the cylinder along the running board varied according to the type or builder's lot. Locations are given below in each of the class notes.

Builders' photos for locomotives built between 1920 and 1949 show an extended pilot deck to allow for installation of flanger blades (it is doubtful ice cutters were used), but until 1947 no flanger blades are shown in place (see the photograph of NR 1021 on page Nfld-15). However, the framework for the blades does appear in photographs taken between 1935 and 1956. The blades were either supplied by the builder or made and installed by the railway. The blades were removed in summer and it appears that, when CNR operated the line, they were not used at all. CNR built three flanger cars on flat car frames, which may have played a part in eliminating the need for locomotive-mounted flangers. All dates are mm-dd-yr.

CNR 15-17 — 4-6-0 TEN WHEEL TYPE 3'6" — second F-3-a

Cylinder	Gear	Driv.	Pressure	Boiler	T.E.	Haulage	Steam	Stkr.	Drivers/Eng./Total	Water	Coal	Length	Notes
Specifications							Appliances		Weights	Fuel Capacity			
17x22"	S	50"	180#	ST	19455		sat		74/ 91/147000	2800 gals	5½ tons	- '	[111]
17x22"	S	50"	180#	ST	19455	19%	sat		74/ 89/169250	2400 gals	8 tons	57-7'	[CNR]

Reid-Newfoundland Company – St. John's 1911-1915 — (3) Acquired by CNR 4-01-1949, effective 11-1950

	Serial	Shipped	New as	7-1923	6-1926	Disposition
—	1	8- -11	RNCo 111	NGR 111	NR 111	Sc bf -36 HD
—	2	-11	RNCo 112	NGR 112	NR 112	Sc by -36 HD
15/2	3	4- -12	**RNCo 113**	**NGR 113**	**NR 113**	Sc 12-26-51 HD
16/2	4	5- -12	**RNCo 114**	**NGR 114**	**NR 114**	Sc 12-26-51 HD
—	5	1- -13	RNCo 115	NGR 115	NR 115	Sc by -38 HD
—	6	3- -13	RNCo 116	NGR 116	NR 116	Sc -38 HD
17/2	7	-14	**RNCo 117**	**NGR 117**	**NR 117**	Sc 7- -53 HD
—	8	-14	RNCo 118	NGR 118	NR 118	Sc -38 HD
—	9	-15	RNCo 119	NGR 119	NR 119	Sc bf -38 HD
—	10	-15	RNCo 120	NGR 120	NR 120	Sc bf -38 HD

CNR 15-17 were from a group of eight 4-6-0s ordered in early 1911 and built as **Reid-Newfoundland Company** 111-118, although the total was increased by two in late 1912 to include RNCo 119 and 120. The projected delivery for all eight was scheduled for 1911 and 1912, but construction time was set back to allow for a pair to be finished in each of the years 1911 to 1914. These became the first locomotives built on the island colony. The last two were completed in 1915. They retained their road numbers throughout **Newfoundland Government Railway** and **Newfoundland Railway** operation, although only three were in service by 1949. During the 1920s the cylinder and linkage to operate the pilot flangers were located above the drivers on the right-hand side of the locomotive.

Of the twenty-five 4-6-0s known to have worked Newfoundland's island railways, only five remained in service long enough to be assigned CNR road numbers. One of three with Reid Newfoundland Company heritage was **NR 112** at a water stop at Millertown Jct. during the early 1930s. It was one of seven removed from service by the railway before 1938. [ROBERT R. BROWN PHOTO/AL PATERSON COLLECTION]

NR 114 was in a storage line at St. John's, and if the photograph was taken during 1951, it would appear unlikely to ever acquire a CNR number. From whatever photographic evidence remains, both these coal-burning locomotives appear to be typical of island-built 4-6-0s, with their unique style of pilot, circular number plates, capped stacks and wooden cabs. Newfoundland Railway lettering, barely discernable on 114's tender, was the style of the 1930s, but the small NR tender wafer on 114 was a standard used during the 1940s. [SIRMAN COLLECTION]

CNR 18-19 — 4-6-0 TEN WHEEL TYPE 3'6" — second F-3-a

Specifications							Appliances		Weights	Fuel Capacity		Length	Notes
Cylinder	Gear	Driv.	Pressure	Boiler	T.E.	Haulage	Steam	Stkr.	Drivers/Eng./Total	Water	Coal		
17x22"	S	50"	180#	ST	19455	19%	sat		73/ 92/148100	2400 gals	8 tons	57-7'	[CNR]

The Baldwin Locomotive Works (Eddystone) 1917 — (1) Acquired by CNR 4-01-1949, effective 11-1950

	Serial	Shipped	New as	7-1923	6-1926	Disposition
—	46636	10- -17	RNCo 121	NGR 121	NR 121	Sc -38 HD
18/2	46637	10- -17	**RNCo 122**	**NGR 122**	**NR 122**	Sc 7- -53 HD
—	46638	10- -17	RNCo 123	NGR 123	NR 123	Sc -39 HD
19	46691	10- -17	RNCo 124	NGR 124	NR 124	Sc 1- -50 HD

CNR **18** was one of four locomotives built for the **Reid-Newfoundland Company** as RNCo 121-124. All four retained their road numbers throughout **Newfoundland Government Railway** and **Newfoundland Railway** operation. Although **18** was recorded with a new number and CNR class, it was reported scrapped still wearing number "122", but NR 124 was scrapped before being renumbered into the CNR series. The latter was not included in Clegg and Corley: *Canadian National Steam Power* locomotive totals (p. 19) or the Newfoundland Division roster (p. 67).

L-7-a

CNR 280 — 2-8-0 CONSOLIDATION TYPE 3'6" — L-7-a

Specifications							Appliances		Weights	Fuel Capacity		Length	Notes
Cylinder	Gear	Driv.	Pressure	Boiler	T.E.	Haulage	Steam	Stkr.	Drivers/Eng./Total	Water	Coal		
18x22"	S	48"	180#	ST	22720	22%	sat		126/147/226600	2900 gals	8 tons	58-11'	[CNR]

Reid-Newfoundland Company - St. John's 1916 — (1) Acquired by CNR 4-01-1949, effective 11-1950

	Serial	Shipped	New as	7-1923	6-1926	Ren. CNR	Rs	Disposition
280/2	11	-16	**RNCo 152**	**NGR 152**	**NR 152**	2-07-51	10- -54	Sc 4-22-55 HD
—	12	-16	RNCo 153	NGR 153	NR 153			Sc bf -38 HD

CNR 280 was one of two locomotives built as **Reid-Newfoundland Company 152** and **153**. Both retained their road numbers throughout **Newfoundland Government Railway** and **Newfoundland Railway** operation. During the 1920s the cylinder and linkage to operate the pilot flangers were located above the drivers on the right-hand side of the locomotive. Besides the five remaining 4-6-0s in 1948, **280** was the only other locomotive not converted to oil. It was stored in December 1953 and taken out-of-service during October 1954. It had spent most its last decade of service as the switcher at Port aux Basques, the western terminus of the line.

Half of the Consolidations used on the island were built there, the others by Baldwin. Home-built **Reid-Newfoundland Company** 153, believed to be at St. John's shortly after its acceptance in 1916, had been fitted with a plow befitting winters on "The Rock". [H.L. GOLDSMITH/GEORGE CARPENTER COLLECTION]

NR 152, on the "Armstrong" (manual) turntable at Bishops Falls, likely during 1943, was the only 2-8-0 to be renumbered into the CNR roster. By the time that occurred in 1949, footboards had replaced the vertical stave pilot, the circular number plate had been removed, and raised cab numerals applied. The NR wafer, however, apparently remained on the tender sides until the end of service. [SIRMAN COLLECTION]

Photos of the coal burner as the Port aux Basques switcher can be found in both editions of Lavallée's *Narrow Gauge Railways of Canada*.

CNR 300-301 — 2-8-2 MIKADO TYPE 3'6" — R-2-a

Specifications							Appliances		Weights	Fuel Capacity		Length	Notes
Cylinder	Gear	Driv.	Pressure	Boiler	T.E.	Haulage	Steam	Stkr.	Drivers/Eng./Total	Water	Coal		
18x24"	W	48"	200#	ST	27540		SCH		115/146/248900	5000 gals	9 tons	66-10'	[orig]
18x24"	W	48"	200#	ST	27540	27%	SCH		115/146/248900	4170 gals	2170 gals	66-10'	[oil]

Schenectady Locomotive Works - ALCO 1930 (S-1693) — (2) Acquired by CNR 4-01-1949, effective 11-1950

	Serial	Shipped	New as	to oil	Ren. CNR	Rs	Disposition
300/2	68400	5-26-29	**NR 1000**	-nd HD	-nd	-56	Sc 6-21-57 HD
301/2	68401	5-26-29	**NR 1001***	-nd HD	-nd	-56	Sc 3-05-57 HD

CNR 300 and 301 were built for the **Newfoundland Railway.** Their design, including an extended pilot deck to accommodate a snow flanger, became the standard from which all other NR Mikados were derived. The air-driven cylinder to activate the flanger was above the steam pipe on the right-hand side running board.

NR 1001 at Schenectady during May 1930, the second of two in the first order of Mikados for the NR, was built to a design which was to remain relatively unaltered for the next twenty years, whether the 2-8-2s were built in New York state, Glasgow or Montreal. [SCHENECTADY WORKS PHOTO S-1693-1/ GEORGE CARPENTER COLLECTION]

Coal-burning **NR 1001**, thought to be at Corner Brook about 1938, had retained most if not all of its as-built features and markings, except for the blanking of the cab's forward side windows. [ROBERT R. BROWN PHOTO/AL PATERSON COLLECTION]

CNR 300, at the St. John's diesel shops on August 27th 1955, had acquired the boiler tube pilot in the early 1940s, but alterations made after Confederation included a standard number plate, cab numerals and CNR wafers the size of those used by standard gauge steamers on the mainland. [JOHN D. KNOWLES PHOTO]

CNR 302-303 — 2-8-2 MIKADO TYPE 3'6" — R-2-b

Cylinder	Gear	Driv.	Pressure	Boiler	T.E.	Haulage	Steam	Stkr.	Drivers/Eng./Total	Water	Coal	Length	Notes
Specifications							Appliances		Weights	Fuel Capacity			
18x24"	W	48"	210#	ST	28920		SCH?		117/152/255870	4170 gals	9 tons	66-7'	[orig]
18x24"	W	48"	210#	ST	28920	29%	SCH?		117/152/255870	4170 gals	2170 gals	66-7'	[oil]

North British Locomotive Company (Hyde Park Works) 1935 — (2) Acquired by CNR 4-01-1949, effective 11-1950

	Serial	Shipped	New as	to oil	Ren. CNR	Rs	Disposition
302/2	24297	-35	**NR 1002**	3-50 HD		12-31-56	Sc 5-13-57 HD
303/2	24298	-35	**NR 1003**	2-50 HD	4-03-51		Sc 9-23-57 HD

CNR **302** and **303** were built for the **Newfoundland Railway** as the first lot of four by the Glasgow builder. Schmidt superheating units were believed installed by the builder, although the manufacturer is not named in CNR documents. The air-driven cylinder to activate the pilot flanger was in the same location as in the R-2-a class.

Coal-burning **NR 1003**, in the yard at St. John's within a year or two of its delivery, still retained its as-built vertical stave pilot and tender lettering. The shield at the cab end of the fuel bunker was standard equipment for all coal-burning Ten Wheelers, Pacifics and Mikados during the 1930s and 1940s. [AL PATERSON COLLECTION]

Sometime in the late 1940s NR 1003 was on the St. John's turntable with a retrofitted boiler tube pilot. The lack of a smokebox number plate was a characteristic of all of the North British 2-8-2s. [SIRMAN COLLECTION]

Oil-burning **302**, at Millertown Jct. on June 30th 1956, carried all of the CNR refinements as well as a replacement air reservoir tank. Another difference in the Scottish-built Mikados was the lack of a throttle casing immediately behind the headlight because of a different arrangement of the linkage for the front-end throttle. [JOHN D. KNOWLES PHOTO]

CNR 304 — 2-8-2 MIKADO TYPE 3'6" — R-2-b

Cylinder	Gear	Driv.	Pressure	Boiler	T.E.	Haulage	Steam	Stkr.	Drivers/Eng./Total	Water	Coal	Length	Notes
Specifications							Appliances		Weights	Fuel Capacity			
18x24"	W	48"	210#	ST	28920		SCH?		117/152/255870	4170 gals	9 tons	66-7'	[orig]
18x24"	W	48"	210#	ST	28920	29%	SCH?		117/152/255870	4170 gals	2170 gals	66-7'	[oil]

North British Locomotive Company (Hyde Park Works) 1937 — (1) Acquired by CNR 4-01-1949, effective 11-1950

	Serial	Shipped	New as	to oil	Ren. CNR	Rs	Disposition
304/2	24436	-37	**NR 1004**	10-49 HD	11-07-50	12-31-56	Sc 5-05-57 HD

Three prewar Mikados were built in two lots by North British. Typical in appearance of the third lot, except for the boiler tube pilot and small NR tender wafer, was oil-burning **NR 1006** simmering beside the turntable pit in St. John's during 1950. The linkage to the lifting arms for the pilot flanger, threaded through the right-hand hanging step, no doubt had the potential of being a working hazard for unsuspecting railroaders. [SIRMAN COLLECTION]

After enquiries during June 1937, **304** was ordered by the **Newfoundland Railway** in July. It arrived on the island in 1938. See the superheating and pilot flanger note under 302 and 303 (page Nfld-6).

The lone member of the second lot, 304, at the St. John's roundhouse on September 6th 1954, had been fully "Canadianized" and recently fitted with a new set of brake hangers. [JOHN D. KNOWLES PHOTO]

R-2-b

CNR 305-306 — 2-8-2 MIKADO TYPE 3'6" — R-2-b

Specifications							Appliances		Weights	Fuel Capacity		Length	Notes
Cylinder	Gear	Driv.	Pressure	Boiler	T.E.	Haulage	Steam	Stkr.	Drivers/Eng./Total	Water	Coal		
18x24"	W	48"	210#	ST	28920		SCH?		117/152/255870	4170 gals	9 tons	66-7'	[orig]
18x24"	W	48"	210#	ST	28920	29%	SCH?		117/152/255870	4170 gals	2170 gals	66-7'	[oil] ■

North British Locomotive Company (Hyde Park Works) 1938 — (2) Acquired by CNR 4-01-1949, effective 11-1950

	Serial	Shipped	New as	to oil	Capy ■	Ren. CNR	Rs	Disposition
305/2	24521	-38	**NR 1005**	6-49 HD		10-06-50		Sc 11-15-57 HD
306/2	24522	-38	**NR 1006**	1-48 HD	4163g 2165o	9-25-50	12-31-56	Sc 3-05-57 HD

CNR 305 and 306 were built for the **Newfoundland Railway**. See the superheating and pilot flanger note under 302 and 303 (page Nfld-6).

CNR 307 — 2-8-2 MIKADO TYPE 3'6" — R-2-b

Specifications							Appliances		Weights	Fuel Capacity		Length	Notes
Cylinder	Gear	Driv.	Pressure	Boiler	T.E.	Haulage	Steam	Stkr.	Drivers/Eng./Total	Water	Coal		
18x24"	W	48"	210#	ST	28920		SCH?		117/152/255870	4170 gals	9 tons	66-7'	[orig]
18x24"	W	48"	210#	ST	28920	29%	SCH?		117/152/255870	4170 gals	2170 gals	66-7'	[oil]

North British Locomotive Company (Hyde Park Works) 1941 — (1) Acquired by CNR 4-01-1949, effective 11-1950

	Serial	Shipped	New as	to oil	Ren. CNR	Rs	Disposition
307/2	24667	-41	**NR 1008**	4-50 HD	-nd	12-31-56	Sc 5-03-57 HD

CNR 307 was built for the **Newfoundland Railway**. See the superheating and pilot flanger note under 302 and 303 (page Nfld-6). When CNR assigned road numbers, the NR sequence of 1007 and 1008 was reversed in order to keep all of the North British 2-8-2s together in one group.

NR 1008 was especially noteworthy for two reasons. First, it was the only North British Mikado to make an ocean voyage during World War II across a submarine-infested Atlantic, and second, because in 1950, with NR 1007, it broke the CNR renumbering sequencing of retaining the last two road number digits. Under the road grime on the tender of the bald-faced 1008 at Bishop's Falls on July 24th 1943, was the wartime slogan "Britain Delivers The Goods". [FRED J. SANKOFF PHOTO/SIRMAN COLLECTION]
See Vol. 1, p. 114. for a post-Confederation view of NR 1008 as oil-burning R-2-b 307.

CNR 308 — 2-8-2 MIKADO TYPE 3'6" — R-2-c

Specifications							Appliances		Weights	Fuel Capacity		Length	Notes
Cylinder	Gear	Driv.	Pressure	Boiler	T.E.	Haulage	Steam	Stkr.	Drivers/Eng./Total	Water	Coal		
18x24"	W	48"	210#	ST	28920		SCH?		117/152/253600	5000 gals	9 tons	66-11'	[orig]
18x24"	W	48"	210#	ST	28920	29%	SCH?		117/152/253600	4170 gals	2170 gals	66-11'	[oil]

Montreal Locomotive Works - ALCO 1941 (Q-391) (1) Acquired by CNR 4-01-1949, effective 11-1950

	Serial	Shipped	New as	to oil	Ren.CNR	Rs	Disposition	To
308/2	69444	6- -41	**NR 1007***	7-48 HD	-nd	Wr 2- -56	Sc 4-09-57 HD	**GFCR 308**

The first Canadian-built Mikado, **NR 1007**, was at Bishop's Falls on June 30th 1943. The design followed that of Schenectady of 1930, which included the smokebox-mounted throttle casing and check valves along the side of the boiler. The location of the air cylinder for the snow flanger linkage followed the North British pattern. Returned to a place of prominence on the face of the smokebox, the round red-fielded cast number plate contained the builder's name and build-date around the circumference with road number in the centre. [FRED J. SANKOFF PHOTO/SIRMAN COLLECTION]

CNR 308 was ordered in November 1940 by the **Newfoundland Railway.** An explanation for the change in road number sequence can be found in the note under 307 (page Nfld-9). CNF 308, 314 and 315 were the only members of the R-2-c class to have an air-driven cylinder used to operate the pilot snow flanger located above the steam pipe at the front end of the right-hand running board. In early 1954 **308** lost its cab and pilot wheels in a collision with a diesel road switcher. It was put into storage at Bishop's Falls until repairs were made by the railway. It was sold, along with 327, to the **Anglo-Newfoundland Development Company** (owner and operator of the Botwood Railway until the name change in April 1957) as **Grand Falls Central Railway Company 308.** Both were to replace a pair of aging North British 2-8-2s, numbers 14 and 15. **GFCR 308** acquired the tender from the 15 for the year it was in service before it too was scrapped in 1958.

CNR 309-313 — 2-8-2 MIKADO TYPE 3'6" — R-2-c

Specifications							Appliances		Weights	Fuel Capacity		Length	Notes
Cylinder	Gear	Driv.	Pressure	Boiler	T.E.	Haulage	Steam	Stkr.	Drivers/Eng./Total	Water	Coal		
18x24"	W	48"	210#	ST	28920		SCH?		122/155/255900	4170 gals	9 tons	66-11'	[orig]
18x24"	W	48"	210#	ST	28920	29%	SCH?		122/155/255900	4170 gals	2170 gals	66-11'	[oil]

Schenectady Locomotive Works - ALCO 1941 (S-1853) — (5) Acquired by CNR 4-01-1949, effective 11-1950

	Serial	Shipped	New as	1945?	to oil	Ren.CNR	Rs	Disposition
309/2	69736	10-16-41	**USA 500***	**NR 1009**	6-48 HD	-nd	12-31-56	Sc 5-21-57 HD
310/2	69737	10-16-41	**USA 501**	**NR 1010**	5-48 HD	-nd	12-31-56	Sc 5-03-57 HD
311/2	69738	10-22-41	**USA 502**	**NR 1011**	5-48 HD	-nd	12-31-56	Sc 5-21-57 HD
312/2	69739	10-24-41	**USA 503**	**NR 1012**	7-50 HD	-nd	12-31-56	Sc 3-05-57 HD
313/2	69740	10-29-41	**USA 504**	**NR 1013**	5-50 HD	-nd	12-31-56	Sc 6-11-57 HD

USA 500, the first of five built at Schenectady during October 1941, was the company's second order for Newfoundland, although they worked for a time on the island under army guises. Retained was the smokebox throttle housing, but the cylinder location to operate the pilot flanger was moved to the left-hand side.
[SCHENECTADY WORKS PHOTO S-1853/GEORGE CARPENTER COLLECTION]

CNR 309-313 were ordered during May 1941 by the **United States War Department** and lettered "**United States Army**" for service on the island. They were the first Mikados to have the pilot flanger cylinder mounted on the left-hand side of the locomotive.

As the Nazi expansion in western Europe became more menacing in 1940, the Franklin Delano Roosevelt administration began to make exceptions to the country's neutrality legislation. Beginning in September 1940, the

(text continues on next page)

CNR 309, in classic CNR form, was sharing space with R-2-a 300 in St. John's yard beside the turntable pit on August 27th 1955. "Oiling around" appears to have been in progress, judging from the oil cans sitting on the pilot deck and beside the rear driver.
[JOHN D. KNOWLES PHOTO]

US Army initiated arrangements to sell and ship large quantities of surplus military equipment to Britain. In exchange, the US was granted rights to establish naval and air bases in Newfoundland, and other British island possessions in the Caribbean. The arrangement developed into what was known as lend-lease, and the concept was the basis of the Lend-Lease Act of March 11th 1941. It also authorized the president to make war and support material available to the government of any country whose defence he deemed vital to the defence of the United States.

Built as part of the Lend-Lease agreement to aid the transportation of war material and in the defence of the island, the Mikados were eventually turned over to the **Newfoundland Railway** when hostilities ceased.

NR 1011, at St. John's Riverhead station about 1948, was typical both mechanically and in markings of postwar Newfoundland Mikados built in North America. Features included the boiler tube pilot, circular number plate, throttle casing, check valve location, Gothic style numbers painted on the cab, and the small wafer on a tender fitted with an oil bunker. [SIRMAN COLLECTION]

CNR 313 was definitely in transition. At the water spout in St. John's, soon after its conversion to oil in May 1950, it carried its NR plate on the smokebox with its road number removed. The new road number had been painted on the cab in postwar NR style, and its new CNR class had been applied incorrectly, using an upper-case sub-class letter rather than the lowercase. At the time, no livery had been applied to the tender sides. [SIRMAN COLLECTION]

CNR 314-315 — 2-8-2 MIKADO TYPE 3'6" — R-2-c

Specifications							Appliances		Weights	Fuel Capacity		Length	Notes
Cylinder	Gear	Driv.	Pressure	Boiler	T.E.	Haulage	Steam	Stkr.	Drivers/Eng./Total	Water	Coal		
18x24"	W	48"	210#	ST	28920		SCH		120/152/253600	5000 gals	9 tons	66-11'	
18x24"	W	48"	210#	ST	28920	29%	SCH		122/155/255900	4170 gals	2170 gals	66-11'	[oil]

Montreal Locomotive Works - ALCO 1941 (Q-392) — (2) Acquired by CNR 4-01-1949, effective 11-1950

	Serial	Shipped	Planned (1)	(2)	New as	to oil	Ren. CNR	Disposition
314/2	69695	12- -41	NR 1008	NR 1009	**NR 1014**	8-48 HD	11-24-50	Sc 11-15-57 HD
315/2	69696	12- -41	NR 1009	NR 1010	**NR 1015**	4-50 HD	-nd	Sc 6-21-57 HD

NR 1014, the first of a pair in Montreal's second Newfoundland order, was at Bishops Falls during the summer of 1947. Despite the slight fogging in the negative's corners, the configuration of the air cylinder and linkage for operating the pilot flanger can be seen arranged as it was for the MLW order in 1941. The single set of cab windows had become standard beginning with deliveries in 1935.
[SIRMAN COLLECTION]

CNR 314 and **315** were ordered by the **Newfoundland Railway**, the first in April, and the second in May 1941. Original planning assigned road numbers 1008 and 1009 in order to have the series continue on from the 2-8-2s built in mid-1941, but, with the arrival of the first pair of the USA Mikados in the fall of 1941, and their anticipated renumbering into the NR 1000-series, these two on order with MLW were bumped down in the series to become 1009 and 1010. However, with the arrival and potential renumbering of yet another trio of USA Mikados as numbers 1011-1013, the MLW pair was again reassigned numbers at the end of the USA order, finally taking the numbers 1014 and 1015. Some MLW records give road numbers as 1009-1010 for serials #69695-69696. The feature article in *Canadian Railway & Marine World* for June 1942 used the builder's photo of NR 1007 to illustrate the report, thus creating additional confusion about the road numbers used for the order. See the pilot flanger note under 308 (page Nfld-10). Both were taken out-of-service during 1956.

CNR 316-319 — 2-8-2 MIKADO TYPE 3'6" — R-2-c

Specifications							Appliances		Weights	Fuel Capacity		Length	Notes
Cylinder	Gear	Driv.	Pressure	Boiler	T.E.	Haulage	Steam	Stkr.	Drivers/Eng./Total	Water	Coal		
18x24"	W	48"	210#	ST	28920		SCH		122/155/255900	4170 gals	9 tons	66-11'	[orig]
18x24"	W	48"	210#	ST	28920	29%	SCH		122/155/255900	4170 gals	2170 gals	66-11'	[oil]

Schenectady Locomotive Works - ALCO 1944 (S-1927) — (4) Acquired by CNR 4-01-1949, effective 11-1950

	Serial	Shipped	New as	to oil	Ren. CNR	Disposition
316/2	71963	11-11-44	**NR 1016**	6-50 HD	-nd	Sc 8-12-57 HD
317/2	71964	11-11-44	**NR 1017**	7-48 HD	-nd	Sc 7-01-57 HD
318/2	71965	12-04-44	**NR 1018**	9-49 HD	-nd	Sc 7-22-57 HD
319/2	71966	12-04-44	**NR 1019**	9-49 HD	10-20-50	Sc 9-17-57 HD

R-2-c

CNR 316-319, built for the **Newfoundland Railway**, were financed by the American Locomotive Sales Corporation. The pilot flanger cylinder was mounted on the left-hand side of the locomotive as were those built in the 1941 and 1944 lots from Schenectady.

Schenectady's fourth order for the island railway was for an additional four coal burners. Converted to oil in 1949, pristine **319** was in the St. John's turntable yard on July 1st 1956. Stencilled with a date of "7-2-1956", the shopping was to be the last, for it had only little more than a year of service remaining. The only departure from the usual appearance was the application of a small CNR tender wafer usually found on rolling stock. [JOHN D. KNOWLES PHOTO]

The firemen of 316, leading a double-headed *Caribou*, was waiting for the departure signal at Humbermouth station during November 1954. One visible change was the relocation of the pilot flanger's operating cylinder to the fireman's side. The angle of view also illuminated the framework ahead of the pilot wheel to which the flanger blade was attached when needed. [ERNIE PLANT/ WES DENGATE COLLECTION]

CNR 320-323 — 2-8-2 MIKADO TYPE 3'6" — R-2-d

Cylinder	Gear	Driv.	Pressure	Boiler	T.E.	Haulage	Appliances Steam	Stkr.	Weights Drivers/Eng./Total	Fuel Capacity Water	Coal	Length	Notes
18x24"	W	48"	210#	ST	28920	29%	SCH		122/155/263440	4270 gals	2170 gals	66-11'	[oil] ■

Montreal Locomotive Works - ALCO 1947 (Q-411) — (4) Acquired by CNR 4-01-1949, effective 11-1950

	Serial	Shipped	New as	to oil	Ren. CNR	Capy ■	Disposition
320/2	75635	11- -47	**NR 1020**	12-47 HD	-nd		Sc 7-01-57 HD
321/2	75636	11- -47	**NR 1021***	12-47 HD	-nd	4163g 2165o	Sc 11-29-57 HD
322/2	75637	11- -47	**NR 1022**	12-47 HD	9-13-50		Sc 10-02-57 HD
323/2	75638	11- -47	**NR 1023**	12-47 HD	-nd		Sc 7-01-57 HD

CNR 320-323, built for the **Newfoundland Railway**, were the first oil burners to be delivered to the island. They were also the first Mikados from MLW to have the pilot flanger cylinder mounted on the left-hand side of the locomotive.

NR 1021 (321) was one of the four post-War Mikados delivered by MLW with pilot flanger blades installed.
[MLW PHOTO Q-411/ FROM *NARROW GAUGE RAILWAYS OF CANADA*, RAILFARE COLLECTION]

They were also the first new oil burners on the island. The first conversion (NR 4-6-2 591) also took place in late 1947, and was followed by a changeover program for the entire Mikado and Pacific fleet beginning in 1948. On a summer's day about 1954, a hostler at the St. John's engine terminal had just moved **320** away from the fuel dock and activated the blower. The railway's oil storage tank overshadowed both the steamer and the fuel dock.
[RAY CORLEY/DON McQUEEN COLLECTION]

The pilot flanger cylinder of 321, at the St. John's diesel shops about 1956, was located on the fireman's side, similar to those in the 1944 order from Schenectady. [DON McQUEEN COLLECTION]

CNR 324-329 — 2-8-2 MIKADO TYPE 3'6" — R-2-d

Specifications							Appliances		Weights	Fuel Capacity		Length	Notes
Cylinder	Gear	Driv.	Pressure	Boiler	T.E.	Haulage	Steam	Stkr.	Drivers/Eng./Total	Water	Coal		
18x24"	W	48"	210#	ST	28920	29%	SCH		122/155/263440	4270 gals	2170 gals	66-11'	[orig oil]

Montreal Locomotive Works - ALCO 1949 (Q-419) $82,063 — (6) Acquired by CNR 4-01-1949, effective 11-1950

	Serial	Shipped	In Service	New as	Ren. CNR		Disposition	To
324/2	76333	4- -49	5-25-49	**NR 1024**	-nd		Sc 8-23-58 HD	
325/2	76424	3- -49	5-25-49	**NR 1025**	-nd		Sc 9-17-57 HD	
326/2	76425	3- -49	5-19-49	**NR 1026**	-nd		Sc 8-30-57 HD	
327/2	76426	3- -49	5-30-49	**NR 1027**	-nd		So 4-09-57 HD	**GFCR 327**
328/2	76427	3- -49	5-18-49	**NR 1028**	-nd	Wr 2-56?	Sc 12-12-57 HD	
329/2	76428	3- -49	5-27-49	**NR 1029**	2-21-51		Sc 11-29-57 HD	

The second lot of MLW's postwar Mikados were to be the last new steam built for Newfoundland service. Within two years following Confederation, all had been renumbered using standard CNR number plates and raised cab numerals, but mainland-sized tender wafers apparently were generally not in use until 1953. Outside the St. John's diesel shops on July 1st 1956, 329 had been released for service without any tender herald, but as with all island steamers during the period of CNR operation, 329 retained road number glasses on the sides of the headlight rather than being fitted with the triangular style of lamp used by standard gauge locomotives. Another departure from mainland standards was to paint the ends of the bumper beam red, a British practice which added to the charm of black locomotives, especially with red-fielded cast number plates and tender wafers. An excellent source of colour images of these unique narrow gauge locomotives can be found in Holland's *Canadian National in the East* (vol. 1). [JOHN D. KNOWLES PHOTO]

CNR 324-329 were built for the **Newfoundland Railway.** The location of the pilot flanger cylinder remained the same as on 320-323 built in 1947. **CNR 328** was involved in two collisions in the 1950s; one, a head-on with NF110 diesel 908 early in 1954, and again, in 1956, a rear-end collision at Cooks Brook which damaged **328** beyond repair. **CNR 327** was sold to the **Anglo-Newfoundland Development Company** (owner and operator of the Botwood Railway until the name change in 1957) as **Grand Falls Central Railway Company 327**. It and 308 were to replace two aging North British 2-8-2s, numbers 14 and 15. **GFCR 327** was sold for scrap to Corner Brook Foundry in August 1958.

CNR 590-595 — 4-6-2 PACIFIC TYPE 3'6" — J-8-a

Specifications							Appliances		Weights	Fuel Capacity		Length	Notes
Cylinder	Gear	Driv.	Pressure	Boiler	T.E.	Haulage	Steam	Stkr.	Drivers/Eng./Total	Water	Coal		
17x24"	W	52"	170#	BEL	20408		SCH?		78/115/199000	3600 gals	9 tons US	62-0'	[orig]
17x24"	W	52"	180#	BEL	20408	20%	SCH?		78/115/199000	3000 gals	1665 gals	62-0'	[oil]

The Baldwin Locomotive Works (Eddystone) 1920 — (6) Acquired by CNR 4-01-1949, effective 11-1950

	Serial	Shipped	New as	7-1923	6-1926	To oil	Ren. CNR		Retired	Disposition	To
590/2	54398	-20	**RNCo 190**	**NGR 190**	**NR 190**	2-51 HD	2-23-51		12-31-56	Sc 4-05-57 HD	
591/2	54399	-20	**RNCo 191**	**NGR 191**	**NR 191**	11-47 HD	-nd	Wr 2-56	12-31-56	Sc 4-23-57 HD	
592/2	54400	-20	**RNCo 192**	**NGR 192**	**NR 192**	11-50 HD	11-29-50		12-31-56	Sc 4-14-57 HD	
593/2	54401	-20	**RNCo 193***	**NGR 193**	**NR 193**	7-50 HD	9-23-50		12-03-57	Dn11-05-58 HD	**C'Brk**
594/2	54466	-20	**RNCo 194**	**NGR 194**	**NR 194**	1-49 HD	-nd		12-31-57	Ss 8-01-58 HD	CMCo
595/2	54467	-20	**RNCo 195**	**NGR 195**	**NR 195**	11-48 HD	-nd		12-31-56	Sc 4-24-57 HD	

Belpaire-equipped **Reid Newfoundland Company 193**, at Eddystone during 1920, was shipped to the island fully decorated with spoke striping and panel trim on both cab and tender. [BLW PHOTO 7859, H.L. BROADBELT/H.L. GOLDSMITH/ GEORGE CARPENTER COLLECTION]

CNR 590-595 were reported ordered with Belpaire fireboxes in November 1920 by the **Newfoundland Railway.** Schmidt superheating units were installed by the builder, although the manufacturer was not named in CNR documents. They were designed with an extended pilot to allow the railway to fit a flanger blade ahead of the pony truck and a cylinder to power the blade which, in the case of the Pacifics, was placed ahead of the cab on the engineer's side of the locomotive. **CNR 590-592** and **595** were taken out-of-service during 1956. **CNR 593** (removed from service in 1957) was donated to the Rotary Club in the city of **Corner Brook** and placed on static display in Lady Bowater Park. **CNR 594**, held for preservation after its retirement, was finally sold as scrap to the **Consumers Metal Company** of Montreal, but the location for dismantling has not been identified, although it may have been Port aux Basques, where it was placed into storage.

Four owners and thirty-seven years later, **CNF 593**, at Bishop's Falls on June 30th 1956, appeared much as when it was delivered, except for the conversion to oil, blanking of the cab's forward side windows, and CNR livery. Although the capped stack was retained, the vertical wood stave pilot had been replaced with one of boiler tubes, and then with a road switcher design combining tubing and kick-plated footboards. Two other 4-6-2s (591 and 597) had similar footboard styles, installed as the Pacifics were displaced from main line service by the Mikados and transferred to branch line and yard service. [JOHN D. KNOWLES PHOTO]

CNR 596 — 4-6-2 PACIFIC TYPE 3'6" — J-8-b

Specifications							Appliances		Weights	Fuel Capacity		Length	Notes
Cylinder	Gear	Driv.	Pressure	Boiler	T.E.	Haulage	Steam	Stkr.	Drivers/Eng./Total	Water	Coal		
18x24"	W	52"	180#	BEL	22880		SCH?		84/124/210400	3340 gals	tons	61-7'	[orig]
18x24"	W	52"	180#	BEL	22880	22%	SCH?		84/124/210400	3340 gals	1665 gals	61-7'	[oil]

The Baldwin Locomotive Works (Eddystone) 1926 — (1) Acquired by CNR 4-01-1949, effective 11-1950

	Serial	Shipped	New as	To oil	Ren. CNR	Rs	Disposition
596/2	59531	-26	**NR 196***	9-48 HD	-nd	12-31-56	Sc 3-05-57 HD

CNR 596 was ordered in August 1926 by the **Newfoundland Railway**. See the note about fireboxes, superheating and pilot flanger arrangement under 590-595 (page Nfld-17).

Oil-burning **NR 196**, rounding a curve with a mixed train at Argentia Jct. on June 19th 1949, was adorned with painted cab numbers and small green-fielded NR wafers. Soon after its delivery, as with all other 4-6-2s, it was fitted for a pilot flanger blade. Unchanged during their years of service (see CNF 593 above), the linkages to the lifting arms on the pilot were threaded through the face of the running board's hanging step. [JOHN A. REHOR/ GEORGE CARPENTER COLLECTION]

CNR 597 — 4-6-2 PACIFIC TYPE 3'6" — J-8-b

Cylinder	Gear	Driv.	Pressure	Boiler	T.E.	Haulage	Steam	Stkr.	Drivers/Eng./Total	Water	Coal	Length	Notes
Specifications							Appliances		Weights	Fuel Capacity		Length	Notes
18x24"	W	52"	180#	BEL	22880		SCH?		87/128/217370	3340 gals	tons	61-7'	[orig]
18x24"	W	52"	180#	BEL	22880	22%	SCH?		87/128/217370	3340 gals	1665 gals	61-7'	[oil]

Montreal Locomotive Works - ALCO 1926 (Q-342) — (1) Acquired by CNR 4-01-1949, effective 11-1950

	Serial	Shipped	New as	To oil	Ren. CNR	Rs	Disposition
597/2	67129	11- -26	**NR 197***	12-50 HD	-nd	12-31-56	Sc 4-23-57 HD

CNR 597 was ordered in August 1926 by the **Newfoundland Railway**. See the note about fireboxes, superheating and pilot flanger arrangement under 590-595, appearing on page Nfld-17.

Similar to its Baldwin forerunner, MLW-built **NR 197** was decked out with trimmed spokes, cab and tender panelling. What is intriguing in this builder's photograph, taken during November 1926, are the blanked-over order and date cards set under the cylinders and cab. They may have been incorrect for the order when photographed. [MLW PHOTO Q-342/H.L. GOLDSMITH/GEORGE CARPENTER COLLECTION]

CNR 597, at the St. John's diesel shops about 1956, had its forward cab side windows blanked and had been fitted with a road switcher pilot. At the time of the photograph the tender carried a small CNR tilted wafer. [DON McQUEEN COLLECTION]

J-8-b

CNR 598-599 — 4-6-2 PACIFIC TYPE 3'6" — J-8-c

Cylinder	Gear	Driv.	Pressure	Boiler	T.E.	Haulage	Steam	Stkr.	Drivers/Eng./Total	Water	Coal	Length	Notes
18x24"	W	52"	190#	BEL	24150		SCH?		91/132/224000	3340 gals	tons	61-7'	[orig]
18x24"	W	52"	190#	BEL	24150	24%	SCH?		91/132/224000	3340 gals	1665 gals	61-7'	[oil]

Schenectady Locomotive Works - ALCO 1929 (S-1644) — (2) Acquired by CNR 4-01-1949, effective 11-1950

	Serial	Shipped	New as	To oil	Ren. CNR	Rs	Disposition	To
598/2	67941	5-24-29	**NR 198***	4-51 HD	-nd	12-31-56	Sc 3-28-57 HD	**GFCR 598**
599/2	67942	5-24-29	**NR 199**	10-50 HD	10-18-50	12-31-56	Sc 3-28-57 HD	**GFCR 599**

J-8-c

CNR 598 and 599 were built with Belpaire fireboxes for the **Newfoundland Railway.** See the note about superheating and pilot flanger arrangement under 590-595 (page Nfld-17). Both Pacifics were removed from service in 1956, but sold the next year to the **Anglo Newfoundland Development Company** for the Botwood Railway under its newly-created name of **Grand Falls Central Railway Company.** Both served as switchers, replacing GFCR 4-6-0 9 and 2-6-2T 10. Photos of the latter can be found in Lavallée, (ed. Ritchie) *Narrow Gauge Railways of Canada* (2005) pp. 82-84. During the year spent on the shortline, **598** lost its pilot truck (making it an 0-6-2) and used the tender of GFCR 9. **GFCR 598** and **599** were both sold for scrap in August 1958 to the Corner Brook Foundry.

Nine years after the initial order for 4-6-2s, panelling and spoke striping was still in fashion with the railway. **NR 198,** with a wood stave pilot, extended pilot deck and two-windowed cab was photographed at Schenectady during May 1929. [SCHENECTADY WORKS PHOTO S-1644/GEORGE CARPENTER COLLECTION]

CNR 598, resplendent in CNR livery at the St. John's engine terminal on August 26th 1955, was sixteen months away from its sale to the GFCR. The Newfoundland Railway had blanked its forward cab side windows and installed a boiler tube pilot, but CNR had converted the coal burner to oil. Check valve location, hand-activated bells and high headlights, either on top of the smokebox, or in the case of the Mikados, on brackets ahead of the smokebox, were common to all Newfoundland's steam power. [JOHN D. KNOWLES PHOTO]